101
DREAM
INTERPRETATION *TIPS*

Jane *Teresa Anderson*

101 Dream Interpretation Tips
First published in Australia by Dream Sight Corporation Pty Ltd
More information at www.dream.net.au

National Library of Australia Cataloguing-in-Publication entry

Anderson, Jane Teresa, 1954- .
101 dream interpretation tips.

Includes index.
ISBN 9780980415704 (pbk.).

1. Dream interpretation. 2. Dreams. I. Title. II. Title :
One hundred and one dream interpretations.

154.634

Distribution in Australia and New Zealand: Dennis Jones & Associates,
Unit 1, 10 Melrich Road, Bayswater, Victoria 3153;
www.dennisjones.com.au +61 03 9762 9100
Cover design: Best Legenz
Internal design: Best Legenz
Project management: Best Legenz www.bestlegenz.com.au
Produced in China by Bookbuilders

CONTENTS

*To my husband, Michael, for sharing
the vision, blessing it with your perfect love,
and living the dream.*

ACKNOWLEDGEMENTS

Across fifteen years of practice, these tips have been tried and tested, developed and refined, by countless dreamers who have chosen to dedicate time exploring their dreams with me. My deepest thanks are extended to you all for the part you have each played in ensuring these tips are powerfully effective and easy to follow. New readers will find their lives changed in wonderful ways, thanks to you.

Thank you to Helen Elward, of Best Legenz, for the eye-catching cover and exquisite page design. You have transformed a bunch of words into a visual feast, a how-to book into a beautiful gift to celebrate or uplift any occasion. Thank you also for your superbly crafted project management and production advice.

Thank you to the Management and Staff at Wenatex, for developing a sensational sleep system that promotes uninterrupted quality dreaming, and for your enthusiastic support in distributing this book far and wide to help people understand their dreams.

Thank you to my family: husband Michael Collins, daughter Rowan Gray, and son Euan Gray, for your unwavering love and support, as always.

And thank you to *you*, the person reading these words, for your interest in this book. A book is just ink and paper until you call it into life by turning the pages.

ABOUT JANE TERESA

Dream analyst and dream alchemist, Jane Teresa Anderson is the author of four paperback books on dreams, including *Dream Alchemy*, and several e-books. She is the creator and writer of www.dream.net.au, one of the most popular dream sites on the net. The site, established in 1998, offers free dream resources, as well as worldwide private consultancy.

Jane Teresa's dream work also extends into the audiovisual media. She is an accomplished dream talk-back radio presenter, having clocked up more than 1,500 radio shows interpreting callers' dreams, and is a regular television guest on local and national television programs in her home country of Australia.

With a Bachelor of Science (Honours) degree in Zoology, specialising in neurophysiology (University of Glasgow, Scotland), Jane Teresa's dream interpretation work brings a balance of the scientific with the intuitive and spiritual.

Jane Teresa began her research into dreams in 1992, involving hundreds of volunteers in her study. She continues to follow her passion exploring new avenues of helping people to live more fulfilled lives by understanding themselves more deeply through their dreams.

INTRODUCTION

When I was a small child, I used to dream of a lake. It was quite an ordinary looking lake on the surface, but if I lay down on the grass and focussed on the edge of the water, something magical happened. I could see inside the lake, from the glistening underbelly of the surface all the way down to the sandy bottom miles below, a breathtaking universe teeming with colourful, tropical fish, quite different from the sombre aquatic life inhabiting the English lakes of my childhood.

Today I live in Australia, a tropical, multicoloured land, where I practise daily the art and science of looking below the surface of the everyday to discover life's deeper wonders revealed in our dreams.

The meaning of my childhood dream was as multilayered as the lake. Was it a glimpse of my future in Australia, or did it inspire me to explore below the surface of the seemingly ordinary to discover the extraordinary power and beauty of life's deeper truths, truths that led me to this place and this work?

In my work as a dream *analyst,* I invite people to look below the surface of how life seems to be, to discover what colours their view of the world and their place in it. In my work as a dream *alchemist,* I then invite them to work a little magic with those colours, to blend or transform them to create new views of their world, and new ways of being in it.

I have condensed the essence of my dream interpretation and dream alchemy techniques into these 101 tips for you to follow. Each tip may look simple on the surface, yet each is multilayered. The more you learn about dream interpretation, the deeper you will see into each tip. At first, you will see simple tips, and for beginners this is perfect. You will learn fast, and be astounded at what you learn about yourself and your life along the way. As you become more advanced in your dream interpretation skills and revisit the same tips over the years, you'll discover gems between the lines—or the tropical fish you didn't see the first times through—and you'll smile, and add another 'Aha' to your wisdom.

Dip into the book at random, use the index to look up what you want to know, or simply start at Tip 1 and read straight through. Enjoy!

1

How to remember and how to record your dreams

Tip 1
Welcome all your dreams

Everyone dreams every night, but not everyone remembers dreams regularly. One thing most likely to turn off your dream recall for many years is fear. One frightening dream can put the stops on remembering your dreams big time. Why is that so bad? Well, you're still dreaming, and probably still dreaming those frightening dreams, but you're missing the opportunity of learning something from them.

When you turn your back on a situation that is worrying you, it grows way out of proportion. When you face that worrying situation and really look at it thoroughly, it's never as bad as it seemed, and you always see a solution in the end. It's the same with scary dreams. To bring back your lost dream recall, be prepared to remember and welcome your frightening dreams because, when you face your fears, you grow.

When you face your fears, you grow

Tip 2
Value your dreams

We all dream. Dreams mostly occur in the REM (Rapid Eye Movement) phase of sleep. If you wake someone up when their eyes are moving rapidly, they will usually report a dream. You can also measure a person's brainwaves while they are sleeping, to chart periods of dreaming. Most people have about five detailed dreams a night.

If you think you don't dream, you're mistaken! In a sleep laboratory, you can let someone sleep their normal number of hours for several nights in a row, but wake them up every time they begin to dream, as measured by brainwave patterns and REMs. After a few days of truly dreamless sleep, people begin to suffer mentally, emotionally, and physiologically, with symptoms similar to the DTs. Dreams are vital for your health and wellbeing.

So it's not dreaming you need to practise, it's remembering your dreams. You may have made a habit of not remembering them. This commonly happens in childhood when you have a nightmare and your parent soothes you by telling you it was "just a dream", nothing to worry about, something to forget. Alternatively, a bad dream or two earlier in your life may have been sufficient for you to switch off recall yourself.

Remembering your dreams is a habit you can learn, and you've made a good start by picking up this book. The more you read about the importance of dreams the more you are likely to take your dreams seriously enough not to dismiss them as soon as you wake up. If you read all the tips in this book, you'll soon remember plenty of dreams.

Remembering your dreams is a habit you can learn

Tip 3
How to catch a dream

ou know the feeling. You wake up with a whole dream fresh on your mind, but within seconds it fades and completely disappears, or leaves just a whiff of a memory behind. How can a dream just crumble away like that? Is there a cure for dream amnesia?

Remembering your dreams is a matter of practice. Dreams disappear when they're in your short-term memory. The secret is to transfer your dream from short-term into long-term memory as quickly as you can, before short's time is up.

The best way to do this is to speak your dream aloud or write down the main keywords straight away. Tell your dream to your partner, speak it into a recorder, or just tell it aloud to yourself. Your long-term memory remembers the way you tell the dream more than the dream itself.

Another way to beat the clock is to set two alarm clocks, one for the time you need to get out of bed, and a more gently chiming one for ten minutes earlier. When the gentle one nudges you from sleep, turn it off, then lay in the position you think you dream in. Your body holds some of your dream memories, so placing your body in dreaming alignment, instead of adopting your waking-up position, helps you to recall your dreams. Allow yourself to drift in this twilight zone between sleeping and waking, and watch for bits of dreams to surface. Don't allow yourself to get anxious, or you'll wake up. Be gentle on yourself. Let dream memories come or go. When you remember part of a dream, trace the story forward and back, asking, "What happened before this?", or "What happened after this?"

Don't use a snooze or radio alarm. The idea is one gentle nudge from your clock before drifting with awareness until your second clock sounds the wake up call. Better still, beat the clock by waking up naturally, if you have that luxury.

Drift in the twilight zone between sleeping and waking

Tip 4
How to catch the first dreams of the night

Like most people, you probably wake up after a good night's sleep with the final dream on your mind but little recall of the four or more earlier dreams you experienced. The final dream is often the most similar to waking life, set in recognisable types of places, featuring events that make some sort of storyline sense. The first dream of the night is often the most vivid, surreal, and emotional. If you had to rank a night's worth of dreams in order of importance for interpretation and personal insight, that first dream would be a winner. So what can you do to increase your chances of remembering dreams from earlier in the night?

The key is to understand that there are several measurable phases of sleep, and you're at your most wakeful directly after a dream phase. 'Most wakeful' does not mean you'll actually wake up. It just means that if something is vaguely disturbing your sleep then you're more likely to wake up just after a dream than at any other time. This is one reason why you think you dream more on very hot or cold nights when the extremes of temperature interfere with your sleep.

Here's how to use this knowledge to your advantage. Before bed, drink a lot of water, more water than your bladder can hold for an eight-hour sleep. Your full bladder is most likely to wake you up at the end of a dream when you are at your most wakeful. When this happens, lie in bed for as long as you can, tracking back through your mind for any memory of a dream. If you can't remember a whole dream, that's fine. One single symbol or fleeting memory is a good start. Write it down on a notepad by the side of your bed (or in your bathroom). From there forward, it's just practice. The single symbol you recall today soon grows, week by week, into full dream recall.

One single symbol or fleeting memory is a good start

Tip 5
How to choose and use a dream journal

If you're serious about interpreting and understanding your dreams, you need to record them in a journal. Before you panic and start thinking, "When have I got time to write out my dreams every day?", rest assured. There are many tips throughout this book suggesting short cuts and ways to economise on your time. For example, when you get proficient at remembering your dreams, you might find recording five dreams a morning impractical. A tip for when you reach that stage of recall is to record just one dream a night, or one dream a week. You'll find tips detailing how to record just one line for each dream too. But if you are just beginning to learn the art of interpreting your dreams, please take the time to record as many as you can remember. Dive in, get plenty of experience, and then choose shortcut methods of recording later, when you have a firm grasp of the basics of dream interpretation.

There are many ways to record your dreams. Most people find a handwritten journal best. For this, buy a beautiful notebook to use as your dream journal, or buy a plain one and embellish it to make it special.

If you prefer to type, simply set up a folder on your laptop. or buy an e-dream journal on CDROM with extra features such as a search facility you can use to search back over your dreams looking for symbols or recurring themes.

If you don't like writing or typing, you can record your dream onto audio, or draw stick figures with speech balloons and linking texts, like a storyboard for a movie.

Record the date and give each dream a title. It's best to choose a title that describes the dream in a nutshell, like 'Lost in the city' or 'Breakfast with an elephant'.

Whichever method you use, leave plenty of space for writing notes later in the day when you revisit your dream to interpret it. You might want to draw up two columns, one to jot down your interpretations, one to note your daily experiences, thoughts, feelings, and issues to see how these reflect in your dreams.

Finally, create an index page at the back of your dream journal, or use a small index book if you are working in audio. Simply list your dream titles alongside their page numbers on this page. Every six weeks, turn to your index page and just read your dream titles in date order. You'll be surprised at how insightful this exercise is.

Or draw stick figures with speech balloons and linking texts

Tip 6
Train your brain

So you wake up and discover zero dream-recall and think, "I'm free! No dream journal writing today!" Wrong. Record something in your dream journal every day. It's important to do this as it creates the habit and helps train you to recall your dreams. It can also be very insightful. But what should you write? Here are some suggestions.

How did you feel when you woke up? Write about your waking feelings, as these are often a hangover from your forgotten dream. Write about how your feelings relate to the last couple of days. If you're unhappy with this feeling or with your situation, finish with a sentence stating how you would like to feel when you wake up, and how you would like your situation to be. Write this sentence under the heading: 'A new day'. There's one proviso: write this sentence in the present tense; for example: 'A new day: I feel inspired and excited', or 'A new day: I have a wonderful job'.

If you can remember a fragment from your dream, or a single symbol (plane, dog), a situation (waiting for a bus), or a feeling (confusion) write, "Once upon a time there was a plane ...", or "Once upon a time I was waiting for a bus ...", or "Once upon a time I was feeling confused ...", and just let a few sentences flow from there. Write fast, without putting any thought into it. Don't judge what emerges. No one is going to read it except you. More often than not, your unconscious mind adds some of the issues covered by your dream into your writing, simply triggered by the dream fragment introduction.

Both these exercises get you closer to your dreaming mind, and train your brain to wake up with better dream recall.

Your waking feelings are often a hangover from your forgotten dream

Tip 7
Recording dreams in the dark of night

How can you record those middle-of-the-night dreams without ending up wide awake, unable to get back to sleep? Turning the light on, sitting up in bed, and writing down your dream in full detail is hardly the recipe for an easy slide back into the land of nod, a good night's sleep, or a happy partner if you're sharing your bed. Yet you know how quickly a dream fades away, so what can you do?

First, invest in a pen with a little light on top. They're easy to find, and tailor-made for writing in the dark. Keep your pen-light within easy reach of your pillow, next to a stack of Post-it notes or a small notebook. When you wake up from a dream, lie still long enough to recall three or four main symbols, then jot these keywords down. This will take only a few moments, not long enough to disturb your sleep. In the morning, you'll discover that those three or four words magically prompt recall of your dream. Then it's time to take your dream journal and write out the full version.

If you're tempted to forgo buying a pen-light, think again. Co-ordination in the middle of the night is not so hot, and what feels like writing on separate lines in the dark often results in an overwritten, illegible knot of a scribble when viewed in the morning.

Occasionally you may wake up to find words etched on your pad with no memory of writing them, let alone any connection to a dream. Once you've checked the handwriting and you know your partner hasn't enjoyed a little joke, simply record the words in your dream journal, or treat them as dream fragments and apply the exercise detailed in Tip 6.

You know how quickly a dream fades away, so what can you do?

Tip 8
Let it flow—slippery secrets revealed

Sometimes it pays not to think too hard when writing about your dream in your journal, recording it in audio, or recounting it to a partner or friend. Let loose a little with your handwriting or typing; speed it up and don't worry about spelling mistakes, grammar, or typos. When telling someone about your dream, don't think about tidying it into a story, or adding humour. Instead, let it tumble out without edit. Why?

When you're not focussing on ordering your thoughts, your dream flows more naturally and you'll find yourself remembering parts of the dream you had forgotten. More importantly, though, when you let go and let flow you'll find slips of the tongue (Freudian slips) and typos reveal clues about the dream's meaning.

Dreams tell their stories in the language of the unconscious, so when you are talking or writing about a dream, or describing its symbols, the language of your unconscious is already on your fingertips or lips. You might look back on your notes and see you wrote 'heal' instead of 'heel', for example. Talking about dreams provides the best of slippery conditions for birthing a telling Freudian slip, making interpretation easier. Look at these examples.

1. "He drenches my thirst."
   Rather than being satisfied (quenched), this person feels she is drowning in her lover's attentions.

2. "She's past her use me date."
   He meant 'past her use-by date', but his slip reveals he felt used by her.

3. "I have to deal with huge clouds of people in my job."
   The issue wasn't about crowds of people. It was about their
   negativity clouding his day.

So write or talk about your dream at speed to create a slippery
surface for your fingertips or tongue. Then write down any typos
or Freudian slips, and ask what your unconscious mind was really
saying about your dream.

*Slips of the tongue and typos
reveal clues*

Tip 9
Too busy? The one-liner method

If finding the time to keep a dream journal is too difficult, then instead of writing down all the details of your dreams, just record 'one-liners'. To do this, take a moment when you wake to recall and review your dreams, and then decide on the one-liners. Keep a journal by your bed, and write them down before you get up.

Here's an example.

Your dream

"A man is showing me a picture in a book. It's dark, and I can't make it out. He starts describing it to me. I feel faint. I feel myself fading out, collapsing to the floor.

Next, I am in a hospital. They tell me I have been in a coma. A doctor shows me an X-ray of my heart. I see a dark patch. His words sound muffled. I think he is telling me my ears are blocked. A nurse comes to syringe my ears, but I am frightened of the syringe, so I pretend to fall asleep."

One-liner

I am choosing not to see or hear something.

Every six weeks, look back through your journal and read the one-liners in date order, like a story. You will see patterns upon patterns, cycles within cycles, new insights, turnarounds, breakthroughs and, running through it all, clues on how to make helpful changes.

Give it a whirl. Let the patterns directing your life today teach you how to change them for a better tomorrow.

You will see patterns upon patterns,
cycles within cycles

Tip 10
Create your personal dream dictionary

uying a dream dictionary from a bookshop is not really going to be very helpful to you because most dream symbols are personal to the dreamer. An elephant in Joe's dream might mean something completely different to an elephant in Matt's dream. Joe might be a cartoonist who learned his first cartooning skills drawing an elephant character, so an elephant in his dream might symbolise 'practice' or 'new skills'. Matt might have been upset as a child to see an elephant trapped in a small cage at the zoo, so an elephant in his dream might symbolise 'trapped' or 'helpless'.

There are plenty of tips throughout this book to help you discover the meanings of your very personal dream symbols, so consider compiling your own dream dictionary. The easiest way to do this is to buy a notebook or journal with A–Z page tags, and enter your symbols as you discover them.

When you record your dreams over the months and years, you'll notice that they recycle many of your symbols, so you'll find yourself consulting your personal dream dictionary frequently.

Make writing your dictionary easy by adding just one or two symbols a day. It will soon build up into an invaluable reference, one you will use for many years to come. Start it today!

Most dream symbols are personal to the dreamer

Tip 11
Create your dream alchemy practice book

hen you interpret a dream, you discover something about yourself and the way you see your world. Depending on what you discover, you may decide you want to make some changes in the way you approach life, so that life delivers you more rewards.

A powerful way to do this, once you've interpreted a dream, is to take a symbol or scene from your dream and visualise transforming it. What this does is transform the way your unconscious mind works, and this in turn transforms the way you see the world, and the way the world responds to you. In other words, life takes a turn for the better, and you attract the rewards you desire.

So, in addition to the dream journal that you need to record and interpret your dreams, you will need a smaller notebook to record the visualisations you decide to do. Don't panic at this stage! As you read the tips in this book, you will gather many suggestions and ideas for suitable visualisations, and similar exercises you can do to turn your not-so-good dreams into wonderful-dreams-come-true. This tip is about getting properly set up so that you will benefit from following through on your interpretations.

Call this smaller notebook your 'dream alchemy practice' book. Practising alchemy is the name of the game: it's all about transforming your dreams and your life into gold. It's a good idea to buy a special notebook for this, something that gives you a feeling of magic and all the good things in life. Handmade paper pages with an exquisite, handcrafted cover would be appropriate. As you do your visualisations and experience the rewards they bring, you will grow to love and treasure this little book, which is why it's important to choose something beautiful and personal.

The reason you need to record your dream alchemy practices is that you need to repeat them over a set period, so regard this little magic book as your recipe book to remind you what you need to do, how often, and when. For example, the best formula for doing your visualisation is twenty times a day for the first week following the dream, ten times a day for the second week, and twice a day for the next month. Use this little book to write or draw your visualisations, and to keep track of time.

It's all about transforming your dreams and your life into gold

2

Weird symbols

Tip 12
Method 1—The personality question

Throw out any dream dictionaries lurking on your bookshelves. The symbols in your dream are all about you. So how can you discover their meaning? Here's an easy, fun, and accurate way.

Imagine your dream symbol is a tennis ball, for example. Ask, "What is the personality of a tennis ball?" Answer fast. Don't allow time to think. You might say, "Bouncy, happy, team-orientated." I might say, "Can't make up its mind—back and forward, back and forward." Someone else might say, "Catch me if you can!" When you do this fast, your unconscious mind comes up with the right answer for you. So YOUR tennis ball dream might be about bouncy team work, mine might be about indecision, and someone else's might hint at dodge tactics.

Build your own dream dictionary each time you do this exercise and discover the meaning of your personal dream symbols.

The symbols in your dream are all about you

Tip 13
Method 2—Look for clichés

ight, sound, touch, smell, and taste. How many of these do you sense in your dreams? The more practised you become at recalling your dreams, the more you'll notice a whole range of senses, but one thing that most people agree on is sight. Dreams are highly visual. You don't fall asleep to listen to a story. You don't go into the dream state to smell your way through the night. You settle down to a visual feast.

When you interpret a dream, think like a painter. Ask how a painter might communicate without sound, touch, smell, and taste.

One method dreams employ is to express issues and feelings in your life as visual clichés. For example, if you've had a couple of days where you've been 'chasing your tail', going round in circles, getting nowhere, your dream might present an animal chasing its tail. Or if you're experiencing a difficulty communicating with someone, your dream might show a cat with a human tongue hanging from its jaws if you're familiar with the cliché: 'The cat's got my tongue'. Or perhaps your dream has you in a car being 'driven round the bend' by someone, or maybe your dream shows you revengefully setting an angry dog onto someone and then that dog 'comes back to bite you' indicating karma, that you get back what you put out.

Some of the weirdest dream symbols are visual clichés. Keep your eyes open for them. They give you a great belly laugh, and you'll pinch yourself at what a clever-clogs you are to come up with these instant messengers in your dreams.

*Some of the weirdest dream symbols
are visual clichés*

Tip 14
Method 3—Teach an alien

ow weird is weird when it comes to dream symbols? Everyday things like a picture frame, a purse, or a paperclip may not be weird in themselves, but weird in the context in which they appear in a dream. A picture frame would be a weird symbol to meet in the middle of a desert, for example.

One approach to working out the meaning of an everyday item in a weird dream is to imagine explaining its use to an alien. For example, "A picture frame is used to enhance your view of a picture, to draw your attention to it, and to get you to focus on it." From this, you might decide the picture frame in your dream was a perfect symbol for 'focus', drawing attention to something in the dream you needed to focus on.

Or you might explain the use of a purse to an alien, saying, "It holds valuable personal things you need to keep safe, like your ID and credit cards, and the key to your car and home." In saying this, you might decide the purse in your dream was a perfect symbol for 'protecting my personal identity' or 'protecting the key to my personal life and who I am'.

Now it's your turn. Have a go at describing the use of a paperclip to an alien. Different people will come up with different descriptions, but if you have actually dreamed this symbol, and it is fresh on your mind, you will discover that the words you choose provide an amazingly accurate clue.

Here's my take on a paperclip: "It's used to hold pages together in an order that can be changed later." If I had dreamed of a paperclip, I might conclude that it was a perfect symbol for 'temporary arrangement' or 'something that can be changed later'.

The alien might still be scratching his head, but you stand to gain new insight into this everyday world you thought you knew so well!

You'll gain new insight into this everyday world you thought you knew so well

Tip 15
Method 4—A quick chat

When you want to discover the meaning of a dream, engage one of the main symbols or characters in a dialogue, on paper or on your keyboard. This is how it works.

As an example, imagine Fiona's dream.
"I was in town when I saw a dolphin on the other side of the street, gasping for water. I offered help, but he bit me."

Fiona decided to engage the dolphin in a dialogue to get to the bottom of her dream. She followed the method, which is to write or type so fast there's no time to think. If you let your thinking, analysing mind take over, it won't work. When you write fast, letting yourself be silly, your dreaming mind takes over and explains itself. Here's her result.

Fiona: Hello dolphin! How are you feeling?
Dolphin: I feel like a fish out of water.
Fiona: You're not a fish. You're a mammal.
Dolphin: Exactly. I want to be like other mammals, living on the land, but I'm seen as a fish out of water.
Fiona: I know how you feel. Sometimes I don't fit in.
Dolphin: Doesn't it make you spit—um, bite?
Fiona: It makes me angry. And it hurts. I feel unquenched.

Fiona's dream was about recognising her anger about not fitting in.

Now imagine two other dreamers, Kirsty and Tom. Since our dream symbols can be very personal, they might have had these results:

Kirsty

Kirsty: Hello dolphin! How are you feeling?
Dolphin: I'm free! Free! Free!

Kirsty: From what?

Dolphin: I escaped the net!

Kirsty: What net?

Dolphin: The tuna net. Too many of us die in tuna fishing nets.

Kirsty: Won't you die on land? You're gasping for water!

Dolphin: My thirst for freedom is putting me at great risk, isn't it?

Kirsty: I can help. Ouch! You bit me!

Dolphin: I like to be free. Don't get close to me!

Kirsty's dream was about her fear of getting too close in relationship.

Tom

Tom: Hello dolphin! How are you feeling?

Dolphin: I swim with the pod. I'm part of the team. We are as one.

Tom: Ah! My swim team when I was a nipper was The Dolphins!

Dolphin: And you were angry with the swimming instructor, remember?

Tom: He always said I bit back.

Dolphin: Who are you angry with now?

Tom: My employer—the team manager. Ah.

Tom's dream was about recognising that he reacts to his employer in the same way that he reacted to his childhood swimming instructor. He is transferring old baggage.

In reality, it usually takes three or four lines of conversation before your dialogue begins to makes sense, so when you do this with your own dream symbol, persevere through the first few lines, and then you'll strike gold.

Tip 16
Method 5—Speed poetry

It's not often that anyone is encouraged to write bad poetry, but this is one of those occasions. Bad poetry has a knack of making a weird dream symbol declare itself. And it's fun. So when you want to discover the meaning of a symbol from your dream, try this method. This is what to do.

Take ten uninterrupted minutes to yourself—turn off the phones, lock the doors. Take a pen and a piece of paper, or your laptop, and a timer. Write the name of your weird dream symbol at the top of the page. It is the title of your poem. Set the timer for ten minutes, and write your poem.

You must write your poem fast, letting your fingers do the writing or typing with as little input from your thinking brain as possible. The idea is not to think at all, but just to let your unconscious mind flow its bad (or good) poetry onto the page.

It doesn't need to rhyme, though speed poems often come out rhyming. It doesn't even need to make sense. The only thing that makes it a poem is that you mustn't write in sentences. Let your poem flow as words or phrases in separate lines. Here's an example.

Red brooch

A little red brooch
Fell off one day
From a coat
Of a goat
Well a nanny goat really
Nanny's brooch.
"Let's broach the subject,"
She said
Of red
Coz it's said
Or I read
That a shed … (continued for ten minutes).

When your ten minutes is up, look over your poem. Whether it turned out to be good or bad poetry, the meaning of your dream symbol will probably jump out at you. In this example, the poem reminded the dreamer of secret meetings he held with his friends in the shed at the bottom of his garden when he was a child. They wore red badges under their lapels. He decided the red brooch symbolised 'secret'.

Your turn!

Tip 17
Method 6—Word association game

Bust the meaning of a weird dream symbol by playing the word association game. For this, you need a piece of paper, a pen, a few minutes of uninterrupted peace, and a timer.

Write your dream symbol at the top of your page, set your timer for two minutes, and jot down the first word that comes into your head when you think about your symbol. Quickly follow this by the next word that comes into your head, and then the next, and so on. Don't think, don't pause, and write fast. It doesn't matter whether the words you write all spring directly from thinking about your dream symbol, or whether they follow on from some of the other words flowing onto your page. Keep going until your two minutes is up.

Imagine your dream symbol is 'hairpin', for example. You might start something like this.

Hairpin, hairpin bend, mountain road, treacherous, treachery, treason, Guy Fawkes Night, fireworks, explosions ... (continuing for two minutes).

When your two minutes is up, look over your list and see if anything significant jumps out at you. If you've really written fast, your unconscious mind will have come up with some surprising connections. This method teases the meaning of your dream symbol from your unconscious mind. Think of it as a kind of surprise attack.

In the example, you might look back over the words and suddenly remember being eight-years-old and taking a hairpin from your hair to dig out some of the explosive from a firework. Your parents didn't notice the firework had been tampered with, they lit it, and it exploded sideways, narrowly missing burning the family dog. Your hairpin dream symbol suddenly feels right as a perfect symbol for guilt.

This example may sound silly, but when you do this exercise, you'll know when you've identified your symbol correctly because it will feel so right, and your dream interpretation will suddenly make sense.

Give it a go. It takes just two minutes, it's fun to do, and it usually yields surprising results.

Tease the meaning of your dream symbol from your unconscious mind

Tip 18
Method 7—'Spot the theme' treasure hunt

ne way of working out the meaning of a weird dream symbol is to hunt the rest of the dream for individual words that play on a theme. It's simple to do and hard to explain, so the easiest way to understand this is to follow the example.

Weird dream symbol
Red shark

Marc's dream

"A red shark is swimming in a pool. A child wearing a 'Save the Whales' t-shirt has taken an interest in the creature. He seems to think the shark is a whale. He wades out into the pool until he is up to his neck in water. I am terrified the shark will hurt him. A man in a vest offers the boy the loan of his fishing net to catch the shark. He throws it to him from his rowing boat, but doesn't take account of the currents, and loses his balance."

Did you spot the theme? It's finances. Let's start with the obvious finance words. These are *save, interest, offers, loan, net, account,* and *balance.* Once you've seen the obvious words, look for less obvious ones. In this example these are *shark* (loan shark), *pool* (pool your money or resources), *up to his neck* (like 'up to his neck in debt'), *in a vest* (invest), *currents* (currency, current account), and *loses his balance.*

You've worked out that the shark symbolises a loan shark, so why is it red? Red is the colour of debt—'in the red'. So the red shark dream symbol emerges as a loan shark that will get you into debt, or a threat of debt. Marc's dream is about his feelings about his financial situation.

When you see an example like this, it looks ridiculous, but when you look at the dreams you've recorded in your journal, you will be amazed at how many are crowded with words playing on the same theme. Why is this?

In the example, many of the words are visual symbols from the dream (such as *shark, save, net*), but most are words Marc has unconsciously chosen to use to describe his dream when writing it out (such as *interest, loan, currents,* and *balance*). Marc might just as well have written, "is attracted to" instead of "has taken an interest in", or he might have put, "loses his footing", or "topples over", instead of "loses his balance".

When you write out a dream, your unconscious mind often scatters clues into your write-up, so wake up to taking a second look at the words you use to express a dream. It's a profitable exercise.

Take a second look at the words you use to express a dream

Tip 19
Method 8—A bunch of fives

I n one eight-hour sleep, you have about five dreams, whether or not you remember them all. Most people who are good at recalling their dreams remember at least two on a good night, but the thought of interpreting up to five dreams each day can be daunting.

The good news is that all the dreams you have in one night usually address the same issue, so if you start with the one that seems easiest to interpret, you can identify the theme, and then see if it applies to the others.

For example, you might be struggling financially and, after a particularly difficult day, your dreaming mind sets out to process your issues about money. The first dream of the night might look at this from an emotional point of view, perhaps showing you 'up to your neck' in water, almost drowning in tears. The second dream might look at this from an historic perspective, reminding you of past events and experiences that have shaped your approach to finances. The third dream might look at how you're coping from a practical point of view, perhaps showing you propping yourself up (with loans or distractions) whenever the ground feels unstable. The fourth dream might get creative, looking for possible solutions to your present crisis, and so on.

As you can see, any one dream on a night gives you excellent insight into any issue, but you can magnify this insight if you explore the other dreams of the same night. If you only ever remember one dream, don't worry. You're not missing out. That one dream provides insight, and there will be other dreams on other nights. It's a good idea to watch a run of dreams over a period of days, or even weeks, before making a big decision, to allow the opportunity to gather a range and depth of insights.

Do you enjoy doing crosswords? If so, you'll probably have noticed that the best approach is to flick through all the clues looking for one you can answer quickly. When you've entered all the answers that jumped out at you, it's easier to solve the harder clues because you now know some of the letters. It's the same with looking at a night's worth of dreams. Start by identifying the theme of the easiest one, then look for clues on the same theme in the other dreams. The more clues you solve, the easier it gets.

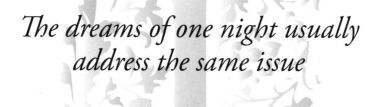

The dreams of one night usually address the same issue

3

Common dream themes

Tip 20
Slo-mo with glue feet

ave you ever dreamed of trying to walk or run somewhere, only your feet feel glued to the ground, or the air around you seems viscous and sticky, making what should be an easy pace into an intense gym workout? You have? It's a very common dream theme. So what does it mean, and why is it so common?

This kind of dream tends to come up when you're resisting progress with something in your life, usually a goal you've been working on, perhaps at work, or in your relationship. Commonly it may relate to someone else's expectations of what you 'should' be achieving, and your dream shows your resistance to this, consciously or—more likely—unconsciously.

When you have this dream ask what, in your life, seems delayed or slowed, and ask yourself what doubts or fears you might be holding onto, or why you might be hesitating. Look for clues in the rest of your dream.

What doubts or fears might be holding you back?

Tip 21
Losing teeth

osing teeth is one of the most common dreams, and many people take it as a dream tip to book a dental check-up, or wonder whether a little too much grinding and gnashing of teeth during stressful sleep is the root cause. Investigate the state of your dental health if you wish, but if you really want to get to grips with the meaning of this dream, think back to your childhood.

One thing we all experienced in childhood was losing our milk teeth, enduring several years, on and off, of gap-toothed smiles and lisping speech, not to mention the painful prospect of having a dangling tooth yanked out by an insistent adult. Common memories of those years include not being able to speak clearly, being misunderstood or made fun of by well-meaning adults, and struggling to be taken seriously while being treated like a child.

Today, when you feel you are not getting your message across to someone, or when you feel someone is not listening to you or is treating you like a child, you may have this dream.

Here's the tip. In your dream, who are you trying to communicate with, or what authority leaves you feeling less than equal, like a child? What else are you losing in your dream, apart from your tooth—confidence, inner strength, conviction, resolve, equality, personal power, self-respect, faith, or face, perhaps? Then ask if you fear or feel you are losing this in your waking life, and what changes you can make to build and grow new strengths.

Are you getting your message across?

Tip 22
Tsunamis and tidal waves

ou don't need to live in a country threatened by tsunamis, or to have seen tidal wave disasters on the news, or to worry excessively about global warming raising sea levels, to have this dream. Seeing or running away from a fast approaching tsunami is a common dream scenario that has plagued people throughout the world, and well before the advent of media images to fuel anxiety and imagination.

When you have this dream—or, more accurately, when you wake up from it and have time to realise you're safe—ask what seems massively overwhelming, like a tsunami, in your life right now. Ah, now this is a bit of a trick question because a common answer to this dream is, "Nothing. Everything's cool." But think again. What's usually happening here is that everything's cool because you believe you're in control. Nothing can overwhelm you. Not even those huge emotions that you're so good at keeping in check. Can you see where this is going?

Emotions and feelings are like waves. We even talk about waves of anger, love, joy, grief, and depression. The truth is that you can't keep emotions in check forever. Those waves of emotions just keep on coming and growing until, one day, they reach the size of a tsunami and nothing is going to stop them, not even you! The secret is to face your emotions while they're little waves, feel them, acknowledge them, see where they're coming from, deal with the underlying issues, and then notice how they dissipate as your inner ocean calms once more.

So what can you do when you have this dream? Is it too late for true emotional calm? Is there no escaping being knocked flat by an unacknowledged emotional deluge? It's never too late. The moment you turn round and face that wave, you begin to slow the momentum. Every moment counts. Your dream tsunami is crying a wall of water to get your attention. Give it the attention that it—and you—deserves right now.

Also see Tips 35, 55, 59

Emotions and feelings are like waves

Tip 23
Naked in public

W hether you're totally naked, missing a top or bottom, or wearing something too skimpy to cover the bits you usually cover up in public, this revealing dream is more about baring your soul than baring your body.

How do you feel in this dream when you suddenly realise you're naked in public? Most people feel embarrassed, or inadequate, but some feel free and elated. How you feel in the dream is a guide to how you feel about finding your true self exposed in public.

If you feel embarrassed in your dream, ask why embarrassment might be holding you back from expressing your true self in public in your waking life. If you feel inadequate in your dream, ask why you feel inadequate about revealing your true nature. When you answer this question, don't think 'body' ("I'm embarrassed about my cellulite."), think 'soul' ("I'm embarrassed that I'm not the person people seem to think I am.").

If you feel fantastic and free with your dream nakedness, think about revealing more of your personality and soul in day-to-day life.

This dream urges you to become more comfortable with your true self, regardless of how other people choose to see and judge you.

The naked body or the naked soul?

Tip 24
Discovering extra rooms

ou're in a house, you open a door, and your heart leaps with surprise. How did this room get here? You never knew it existed! How could you have passed by this way so many times and never seen this door?

The house may be familiar to you from waking life. Or it may be a dream house you thought you knew intimately until you discovered this extra room. How would you describe this room? Is it brand new, an extension of the old home? Or is it old, perhaps decorated in the style of a past era, or abandoned and covered in spider webs? Is it empty, a blank canvas inviting you to put it to use? Or does it hold secrets: scary, frightening secrets that make you want to slam the door and get out of there fast, or enticing secrets that may provide the answers you have been seeking?

The tip here is to ask these kinds of questions until you discover the feel and age of this room. For example, you might say, "1970s, abandoned" or "brand new, expansive" or "ancient, scary". Houses in dreams often represent your mind or self, the rooms being different areas of your mind or self. This dream comes up when you suddenly discover an area of your mind and self you didn't know existed, or one you have firmly shut from your conscious memory. Knowing the feel and age of your dream room is a huge clue to identifying this newly discovered opportunity for you to grow and expand, to fulfil the potential of this area of your mind by using or transforming it in whichever way you wish.

So your dream room was '1970s, abandoned'? What did you abandon in the 1970s, or did you feel abandoned back then and close a part of yourself down? So your dream room was 'brand new, expansive'? Great! It's a brand new potential or expansive attitude you've just discovered! Or was your room 'ancient, scary', indicating the potential healing and growth you can achieve by facing that old fear and blowing it away, once and for all?

Also see Tips 62, 79

There's always room for growth

Tip 25
Animal dreams

nakes, whales, jaguars, dogs, cats, rats, exotic or mundane, wild or domestic, animals not only populate our dreams but often take leading roles, sometimes speaking roles, chatting away as if they were human. Usually, though, they communicate in the way animals do, a defensive roar here, an impatient swish of a tail there, a sly slither or wriggle, a cunning foxtrot, a sting in the tail, offering a feather for a nest, an exposed tummy for a tickle, or an elaborate courting ritual.

What do all these animal communications have in common? They're survival instincts aimed at securing food, shelter, territory, mating, offspring, and safety. And that is the tip, the key to why you dream of awesome, even magical animals at certain times in your life. These dreams come up when your basic survival feels threatened.

The cause may be obvious. You may have just lost a job, income, partner, or home, and you may be wondering how you are going to survive—physically, mentally, emotionally, or spiritually. Or the cause may be more subtle, perhaps a feeling that you're losing hard-won territory in a working relationship, or feeling insecure about a big change in your life.

When an animal appears in your dream, ask where in your life you are feeling the pressures of survival.

Sometimes you need to tune into your animal instincts to get through hard times. You might need to get in touch with your animal intuition, be guided by your gut feelings, start building a new nest (home), or work with the pack (team or family) to ensure your needs are met.

Sometimes your natural animal instincts might be working against you, as you snarl and growl to defend your patch (work, mate, space) instead of negotiating a friendly win-win outcome.

Look at the animal in your dream. What are its survival instincts? Which of these instincts could work for you and which against you? What can you learn about yourself and your situation from this awesome animal energy in your dream?

Also see Tip 56

Tune into your animal instincts

Tip 26
Chased or followed

ave you ever been chased in a dream, by a person, monster, or animal, or perhaps simply heard the footsteps of a shadowy figure echoing behind you in undercover pursuit? Have you spent the dream trying to elude your follower, running away, or looking for somewhere to hide or outwit your determined pursuer?

This dream comes up when you've turned your back on something —a problem, event, feeling, or situation—and you are trying to run away from it instead of facing it. Have you ever noticed that you never really get away in these dreams? Even if you do have some success one night, the dream returns, and you'll be ducking and diving and running again. The only way to stop this dream is to face the situation and solve or heal it so there's no longer any threat or need to escape.

You may have enough clues in your dream to work out what this situation is, and why you're afraid to face it, but even without these clues you can do an exercise—a dream alchemy practice visualis-ation —that will quickly and smoothly persuade your unconscious mind to automatically solve this issue once and for all. This is what to do.

When you are awake, close your eyes and imagine yourself momentarily back in your dream, only this time know that you are completely safe because you are awake, just looking into your dream. Now imagine stopping and turning around to face whatever or whoever is chasing you. The moment you do this, see the chaser stop, and see two guardians, or angels, or people you love and trust, walk over to hug the chaser. As they walk towards the chaser, see the chaser change from the form in the dream into a beautiful little child, so happy to receive some love and attention AT LAST! Feel that happiness fill your own body and mind. Imagine walking over and hugging the child too. FEEL the relief of the child in every part of your own body and mind. Peace at last. Do this visualisation 20 times a day for one week, 10 times a day for the next week, then twice a day for the next four weeks.

What will happen is that you will find yourself becoming aware of the issue, knowing what to do about it, and then confidently acting on it.

Turn round, face the situation

Tip 27
Feeding and changing the baby

As a mother of children long out of nappies, or now grown up with children of their own, do you ever dream of those early babyhood days? Do you find yourself changing nappies and feeding your babies in these dreams? Or is it more a case of, "Oh no! I've forgotten about the baby! I haven't fed her for days, and I haven't checked her nappy for hours!"

Of course, this never happened to you, did it? Your babies were loved, nurtured, fed, watered, and dried on time. But were you?

In those busy, whirlwind, mothering days, how often did you feel in need of some extra nurturing, a sleep in, someone to pick you up and cuddle you when you felt like crying or needed attention, someone to cook you dinners, bring you drinks, wash and iron your clothes, keep you looking your freshest and best, entertain you, teach you, acknowledge you, admire you, congratulate you, and take total responsibility for your every desire?

And how often does this apply to you today, even now that your children are grown and flown?

The very common, 'I've forgotten to feed the baby …!' dream usually comes up when you're not paying attention to yourself, not nurturing your own physical, mental, emotional, or spiritual wellbeing.

Ask if you're in the habit of putting other people's needs before your own, and then ask why you feel you're not equally deserving of receiving love.

Isn't your dream clever to show a beautiful baby in danger of neglect? Who could fail to respond? But it is you and your needs that are beautiful and in danger of neglect. Respond.

Also see Tips 40, 46

Whose needs do you put before your own?

Tip 28
A suitable toilet?

ome people say it's probably just as well that most toilets you find in your dreams are unsuitable to use, because otherwise you might end up wetting your bed—or worse. This may be the case when your bladder is bursting and the physical sensation is impinging on your dream creating the whole, urgent, 'Where's the toilet?' scenario. Body sensations can and do affect your dreams, and since most people need to get up and empty their bladder during the night, the common occurrence of this dream is not surprising. However, how many times have you woken from this dream without a pressing bladder? And has your physical bladder ever emptied itself while dreaming of peeing? Probably not. These dreams are common, and symbolically meaningful.

The usual dream scenario is that every toilet, no matter how promising it appears to be, turns out to be unsuitable. Public toilets are locked, or there are no doors or walls on the cubicles, or the toilets are too filthy or overflowing to use. Another variation is that you do get to pee or empty your bowels but you can't get the toilet to flush, or it starts overflowing while you are using it. In more fulfilling toilet dreams, you get to fully and happily relieve your bladder or bowel, sometimes even in public or out in nature, and then continue with your dream with no further pressing need to find a toilet.

The tip for interpreting these dreams is to see emptying the bladder or bowel as releasing toxins and waste products from your system. These are times for letting go of things in your life that need to be let go. When the let go in the dream is easy and good, and the waste products flow away, you are letting go of issues in your dream. Too often, though, we feel surrounded by 'crap' that clogs up the natural flow of life. When this happens, you may dream of overflowing or dirty toilets. And when that 'crap' is building up within you, when you just can't seem to find the right conditions to let it go, you encounter unsuitable dream toilets.

This dream is also to do with not getting enough privacy in your life, particularly for processing and letting go of emotional issues and related 'crap'. There's always the feeling of someone looking in, when all you need is time to yourself. When you have this dream, plan some quality private time, or ask why you feel unable to discuss and process some of your issues in public.

There are times for letting go

Tip 29
Who's driving this car?

 hile you may delight, in everyday life, in taking the passenger seat and letting someone else take a turn at driving, you might like to check who's driving you in your dreams.

A common dream is to be suddenly aware that your car is meandering across the road in the same moment that you realise no one is driving. You are in the passenger seat or, worse still, in the back seat, so you reach over and try to grab the wheel or put your feet on the brakes, or both. Unless you become extraordinarily acrobatic in your dream, this is, of course, impossible.

Ask where in your life today you have vacated responsibility for where you're going. It might be in your relationship, finances, work, health, or fitness for example, but, wherever it is, your dream shows it's time to take back responsibility if you want to have a say in where you're heading.

It may be easier said than done, as you must have abdicated responsibility for your life direction for reasons such as fear, or being overpowered by someone else's wishes, and may not be keen to stand up to these. To help get your life back into control, visualise sitting in the driver's seat of that dream car, relaxed, confident, and loving, your hands on the wheel and the engine purring beneath you.

Another common variation of this dream is where you suddenly realise the car is speeding out of control, crawling to a halt, or taking off in the wrong direction, and you are powerless to do anything about it because someone else is driving.

More often than not, that driver is your father, another authority figure, or someone you have given your power to in daily life. In your dream, that driver represents the 'driving force' in your life. Many people are still driven, in adulthood, by the expectations of their father, for example, which is why dad is most often at the wheel.

Ask what belief the driver has about life. You might say your father believes life is about making money, in which case your dream shows you might also be driven by a belief in making money. If the resultant dream journey is not good, it's time to examine the beliefs that are driving you, as well as the goals you have chosen to make your destination. It's never too late to make a change.

Also see Tips 30, 61, 97

What drives you?

Tip 30
Lost or stolen car

ou know you parked your car somewhere, but where? In this common dream, either you can't remember where you left your car, or there's an empty space where once it stood.

If the car you're looking for is the car you drive today, this dream most likely means you've lost your 'drive', or are close to losing it. Dream symbols often play on words, so your dream car frequently represents your drive or motivation. Have you taken a rest only to experience difficulty finding your drive again?

If the car you're looking for in your dream is one you had in the past, ask what your goals were back in those days. Ask what motivated you back then. Have you lost touch with this goal, or with your old drive? Ask if you would like to introduce it back into your life, or whether this is a time, finally, to let it go. (If you ask the right questions, based on a dream, you'll find your answers come easily.)

If you're looking for a dream car—perhaps you were driving it earlier in the dream—ask what kind of person drives a car like that, or, if that kind of car were a person, what would its personality be? You might say 'vibrant' or 'practical', in which case ask where in your life today you're losing touch with your vibrancy or practicality.

There are times for giving your drive a rest, for relaxing between goals, for spending some time being instead of doing, but if you've had a rest yet seem to lack motivation, this is what to do.

Visualise the kind of car that would take you to the kind of place you would like to be, and imagine walking up to that car in that previously empty dream parking spot, unlocking the door, turning your key in the ignition, and taking off. Keep up the visualisation, and you'll soon find your drive is back.

Also see Tips 29, 61, 97

Have you lost your drive?

Tip 31
Flying

I't's one of the most exhilarating dream experiences, flying up and up, over houses, trees, fields and seashores, looking down on your world from above. At least, it is when you don't get caught in the powerlines on the way up, as many dreamers do. Others don't get that far, spending their dream hovering a few inches above the ground, or taking huge, bouncy leaps like walking on the moon.

Does your dream see you flying high and free, or putting your energy into trying to get off the ground, or freeing yourself from obstacles you meet on the way up?

The flying sensation is so real that many people feel they are having an out-of-body experience, or astral travelling as their spirit leaves the sleeping body and goes visiting in the physical world. If you interpret your flying dreams, however, you'll see they relate to your life, belonging firmly to the realm of the symbolic. So what do these dreams mean?

Flying is usually about reaching a higher potential in some area of your life, lifting yourself to a higher level, finding the wind beneath your wings, taking off, moving on up. If you're flying high and free in your dream, you have no unconscious barriers to achieving this. If you're holding back, trying to persuade others to fly with you, they represent your doubts, so look for clues in your dream to identify those doubts so you can overcome them. If one doubter is a person you know to be shy, for example, ask why your own shyness may be holding you back.

If your dream shows you not quite being able to get off the ground, ask where this seems to be happening to you in your life today, then, whenever you're in that situation during the day, summon up an uplifting, soaring, joyful feeling, as if you're actually flying. It will make a difference deep down inside, and you will surprise yourself with your achievements.

Here's a tip about those powerlines. The very common dream of flying up and getting caught in, or held back by, powerlines usually means there's an issue of power or control in your way. Remember, dreams love playing with words to express a situation. Are you fearful of your own power, or someone else's? Free yourself to fly!

Free yourself to fly

Tip 32
Running late

You're running for the plane, but your passport isn't in order. Or you arrive at the station in time to see your train depart. Or perhaps you look in your diary and you are horrified to discover that your job interview is in ten minutes time and you haven't left the house yet. The theme is being late for—or missing—an appointment, and if you've had this common dream you'll know how upsetting it is because you—of all people—are never late for anything, are you?

It's not just a case of getting the time wrong. All manner of things seem to conspire in these dreams to make you late—too late usually. People ask you favours, ticketing is wrong, baggage is too heavy or goes missing, you can't find addresses, phone numbers, booking slips, or a taxi to speed your journey and make up for lost time. And throughout it all, you feel frustration. At no point do you think, "Oh well, never mind. There's always another time," or "Perhaps there's another opportunity for me somewhere else here." No. It's a do-or-die appointment, and it looks like the latter.

So what does this common dream mean? It's often the dream of perfectionists, which is why it is baffling to dream this scenario when you're never late for anything. When you're a perfectionist, you dread a less than perfect performance. It's do-or-die. There's no in-between. On the one hand, your dream shows your fear of not meeting your deadline and being judged accordingly, while on the other it shows your reticence to put in anything other than a perfect performance. Better to miss the deadline than be seen as less than perfect. What a dilemma!

When you have this dream, ask which goals in your life today seem to be getting further and further away from you. Where are you running behind schedule, late, perhaps wondering if you'll ever get there? Or what goals have seemed to be right there—right in front of your eyes, due for takeoff next week, yet fading away in the next moment? Where do you seem to be just missing out every time you think you are so near? What opportunities seem to evaporate from one moment to the next, no matter how hard you work at achieving them?

Ask what you have to lose by achieving this goal, and what you have to gain by missing it. Be honest. Your answer will reveal what is holding you back, and the details in your dream, once interpreted, will confirm this.

Also see Tip 58

What would you gain by missing the plane?

4

Recurring dreams & nightmares

Tip 33
Groundhog Day

ave you seen the movie *Groundhog Day*, where Phil wakes up each morning to live the same day, over and over again? He's trapped in a recurring daydream. Perhaps he would call it a recurring day-mare. And yet, how many of us repeat the same patterns, attitudes, and approaches to life day after day? If you want change in your life, then you need to make a change, a change in attitude or approach, for example. It's that, or stay stuck, stuck, stuck.

That's where recurring dreams come to your rescue. Recurring dreams—either the same dream or the same dream theme—come up because something in your waking life is happening over and over again. That recurring thing is usually an unresolved issue, attitude, or approach that is keeping you stuck. Since dreams always refer to the last 24–48 hours, keep a diary of your recurring dreams. Look back over the last two days for each repeat of your dream until you identify the linking daytime issue. That's your stuck issue, and your dream, once you've interpreted it, gives you clues about how to make a change that will move you forward and release you from the dreaded Groundhog Day!

Change or stay stuck, stuck, stuck

Tip 34
How to break through a recurring dream

ow many of your dreams have happy endings? How many have satisfactory endings? How many of your dreams seem unfinished? How many end up going round and round in circles, getting nowhere? To put this another way, if you went to the cinema and saw your dreams made into movies, how many would leave you feeling cheated, thinking, "I paid good money for that movie and I sat there and hung in till the end and all for nothing! It just left me up in the air!"

Dreams that don't really have endings are unresolved dreams. They happen when your dreaming brain is still trying to fathom out a solution to a challenge or difficulty you're experiencing in your waking life. Here's a simple exercise you can do to help your dreaming brain find an excellent solution, one that will work its way into your life with positive results.

Imagine waking up from an unresolved dream, knowing that your dream was unresolved because somewhere in your life, something is unresolved. You may not understand what the dream means in detail, and you may not even know to which area of your life it applies. That's okay. You don't need to know this for the exercise to work. Imagine, for the moment, that your unresolved dream was the one where you were walking around a city, completely lost.

Now, imagine yourself back in that dream and introduce a change. Introduce an open door into the dream scene. Make that open door safe and beautiful, perhaps have a loving light emanating from it, or a glimpse of sunshine, or a few bars of uplifting music. Imagine that beyond that open door are all the solutions you will ever need in your life. That's all you need to do in this dream alchemy practice. You don't need to go through the door in your visualisation. It's enough just to notice that it's there, and to know that all the solutions you will ever need are through that door. The door is permanently open, because the solutions are always there. They always have been, and they always will be. You just haven't known that, until now.

You can apply this simple exercise, a dream alchemy practice, to any unresolved dream. Just visualise the most stuck part of the dream, then introduce the open door and all the uplifting, safe feelings that go with knowing it is there.

Do this 20 times a day for two weeks. What will happen is that at some time during the two weeks you will suddenly have an idea or see your situation in a new way. It will seem to come out of the blue, and so it will surprise you. Think about it, consider it, and if the idea or new insight seems good, act on it. You will be well on the way to finding a solution to the situation that, until now, had seemed unsolvable.

Tip 35
Love your bad dreams

ere's a simple formula to apply when you have an unsettling or frightening dream and you want to reduce the chances of having it again. Actually, it's far more powerful than this. Not only does this formula ease your dreams, it also creates deep and lasting positive change in your waking life by subtly reprogramming your unconscious mind to solve the issue causing the bad dreams. Here's what to do.

Love your bad dreams into good ones. Do this by rewriting your dream in your journal, or visualising it in your mind's eye, changing the bad storyline into a good one, making sure that all your changes come from a place of love. Here are some examples.

Love your losses into founds, your deaths into births, your failures into successes, your limitations into freedoms, your lateness into smooth timeliness, your obstacles into open roads, your judgements into forgiveness, your muddy waters into crystal pools, your intruders into friends, your poverty into wealth, your wicked witches into good fairies, your broken-down cars into golden chariots, your tsunamis into relaxing spas, your hurts into healings, your heavy luggage into uplifting wings, and your scary shadows into loving light.

The key is transformation. For example, don't kill a wicked witch because this leaves a hole in your psyche. Everything and everyone in your dreams represents something about you, and your beliefs and feelings about life, so anything you do to anyone or anything in a dream (or a dream rewrite) you are really doing to yourself.

Transform a wicked witch into a good fairy by whatever way feels good to you when you rewrite your dream. Best of all is to use love as the transforming force. When a wicked witch receives love, she can't help but be instantly transformed into a good fairy.

Finish your rewrite with a bit of wisdom and a happily ever after ending. Reread it, or replay it in your mind's eye, over and over again, making sure you feel uplifting emotions and plenty of love throughout. Take that 'happily-ever-after' feeling forward into your day.

Love your losses into founds

Tip 36
Children's nightmares

How can you help your child when she has a nightmare? What frightens young children most is that they believe their dreams are real, so you might think the best thing to do is to reassure them that their nightmare is "only a dream, nothing real", and then try to settle them back to sleep, but it's not. Your child's dream was a very real experience, especially emotionally, so telling her it was not real is very confusing for her. She may hold back from sharing other emotional experiences with you in the future if she feels you might not validate them.

Unfortunately, this approach also has the long-term effect of reducing dream recall as an adult. What you are really doing is saying, "Dreams are not important, so turn off the recall." You are also giving your child the message that she should dismiss her fears as unreal, rather than face and deal with them.

As an adult, you know it is better to face your fears than to bury your head in the sand. You know that fears don't go away. In fact, they grow bigger and more worrying the more you try to ignore them. When you turn and face an issue that has been fearful for you, your fear diminishes, and you find solutions to the problem. You become more empowered to live a whole life, rather than to hide from parts of it. When you acknowledge your child's fear after a nightmare, what you are really doing is teaching your child, in a loving and supportive way, to face her fears. You are giving her a wonderful gift that will empower her through her childhood and adulthood.

Your child's nightmare is part of her process of trying to make sense of her world. When you both can talk about her dream—especially when you, the parent, understand a little more about what her dream means—you can help her overcome her natural and normal fears around her everyday life experiences. By repressing dream recall, you are both missing a wonderful opportunity for her to grow into her world with more ease and wisdom.

The day after her nightmare, encourage her to paint, draw, or act out her dream, but with a changed, happy ending. Help her to wave a magic wand to transform her dream monsters into fun toys, and bad dreams into new stories with happy endings. Stay clear of killing the monsters—the key is to transform bad into good so that she practises the art of transforming life's negatives into positives.

Help your child handle fears

Tip 37
An evil presence

his extremely scary dream usually leaves you absolutely certain that there's an evil presence in your bedroom, but rest assured, this is not true. It's a very common dream, and the reason it feels real is that your body is pumped with the fear hormone, adrenalin, and the scenario is believable because the dream scene is usually similar to the place where you're asleep.

This dream comes up when you are judging and blaming yourself for something, or pretending that you never have negative feelings such as anger and guilt. You see these feelings as 'evil' and separate from yourself (like the separate, evil figure in your dream), but they still haunt you. It's time to stop judging and blaming yourself and your feelings! Here's a dream alchemy practice to stop this dream. It works by gently changing the way you see yourself and the world, eliminating the 'evil' haunting.

Visualise a white light around your body, protecting you from all harm. It is a beautiful, peaceful light, like pure love. When white light shines into a dark corner, it banishes darkness. The corner becomes light and peaceful, pure love. This white light permeates your whole body and mind, as well as surrounding you. You are beautiful in this light. Today, and forever more, you are beautiful surrounded by this light, and it will always be with you, soothing your negative thoughts and feelings, gently showing you the positive side of everything in your life.

Do this visualisation before you fall asleep, whenever you wake up during the night, and just before you get out of bed in the morning. Do this every day for a month. This is such a beautiful practice that you may want to keep it up forever. One month is enough to stop the bad dream: forever adds a special touch to every day and night of your life. One day, you will notice you are no longer weighed down by feelings of guilt, or haunted by negative thoughts. Instead you will notice how compassionate and forgiving you feel towards yourself as you look back on your life experiences.

Also see Tip 38

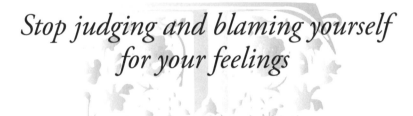

Stop judging and blaming yourself for your feelings

Tip 38
Things that go bump in the night

Ever woken to eerie sounds in the night, or a feeling of your skin being touched when you're sleeping alone, or been scared out of your wits when you've opened your eyes to see ghosts or strange things going on in your bedroom? As utterly convincing and frightening as these sensations are, it's important to take a deep breath and know that what you are hearing, feeling, and seeing is not real. Neither are you going insane.

What you are doing is dreaming while partly awake, so that both your dreaming and waking worlds overlap. You could say you are experiencing the 'Twilight Zone', not a scary spirit world but a brain zone where the night of dreams mixes with the light of day in a hazy, confused half light. This is how it happens.

When you wake up to visions in your bedroom, you are experiencing a phenomenon known as 'hypnopompic hallucination'. When you open your eyes while you are dreaming, your eyes transmit a picture of your bedroom to your brain, and this is then superimposed onto your dream images. Because your eyes are open, your brain decides the mix of images is a real event situated in the bedroom. So you see the ghost, or dream scene, in your room.

The same applies to other sensations such as sound and touch. If you start to wake up while you are still dreaming of a wolf howling, or a tiger nuzzling your skin, your brain will superimpose the fading howls or the warmth of the tiger's breathy lick onto your bedroom scene. You will be absolutely convinced that a wolf is outside your door, or that a tiger is under your bed, as your ears will still be ringing, and your skin still tingling. The sensations feel real, but they are dream sensations, dissolving away as your brain becomes fully awake. The memories of those sensations may haunt you, but they were dreams.

Have you ever got into bed and then felt the covers lift as if an invisible stranger or spirit has just climbed in with you? The explanation for this sensation is the same, except that your dreaming mind has switched on while you are still half-awake. This common experience usually happens when you're not expressing your whole self, holding back too much of the real you, the true enormity of your power. Your dream is about to introduce your 'lost spirit' and you perceive this lost, detached, abandoned shadow as a separate being as your brain begins to switch into dreaming mode.

So when these kinds of spooky events happen to you, relax in the safety of this knowledge, and be amazed at the power of the mind to believe what it sees and feels. Then simply record your awesome 'Twilight Zone' experience, and interpret it as the dream it really is.

Also see Tip 37

Tip 39
Can't shout, frozen with fear

hy can't you scream out for help during a scary dream? At most you might manage a squeaky peep, and, even if you know you are dreaming, it can be so hard to wake yourself up. Related to this, why is it that even when you wake up from some dreams you feel paralysed as if there's an immoveable weight on your chest, pinning you down?

There are two different and quite natural physiological forces at work here. The first one is known as 'sleep paralysis'. When you fall asleep, your brain signals your major motor muscles to more or less stop moving. This stops you from acting out your dreams, and keeps you safely tucked up in bed so you can't hurt yourself. If your mind wakes up from your dream before your brain has released its hold on your muscles, you will find yourself awake and unable to move. It passes within moments, so don't panic. Just breathe easy, and thank your physiology for protecting you while you sleep.

The second type of paralysis, experienced while dreaming or for a few seconds after waking, happens when your body is pumped with the fear hormone adrenalin. When you have a nightmare, your body responds to the fear you feel in your dream by releasing this hormone into your blood in exactly the same way that it does when you are awake and feel fear. This is a normal and natural body survival response, as the purpose of adrenalin is to pump you up for 'fight or flight'.

In pure survival terms (when facing a tiger in a jungle, for example) this means fighting what is frightening you, or running away from it—either way in an effort to save yourself. However, another thing that can happen with adrenalin is that you 'freeze' on the spot. (It's what gives you a cold sweat when you're scared.) You see this in some animals confronted by an attacker. It's as if they're unable to decide whether to fight or run. For some animals, this 'freeze' works to their advantage, scaring away the enemy, because it gives the impression that they're courageously standing their ground.

It's the adrenalin response that gives you goose-bumps when you're really scared, sends your heart rate soaring, and sometimes freezes your voice, in and out of dreams.

So relax, and know that your body and mind are working beautifully as nature intended. Then, if you can remember your dream and it was laced with fear, ask where in your waking life you are feeling overwhelmed, perhaps even paralysed with fear. Look at the details in your dream for clues, and use the dream interpretation skills you are learning in this book to help you get to the bottom of your dream so that you can face and heal that fear.

Thank your physiology for protecting you

Tip 40
A parent's worst nightmare

It's probably the scariest and yet most common dream of any parent. In the dream, your baby son or daughter drowns in the bath after being left unattended for a moment. Or your baby slips down the plughole in the bath or sink, or gets washed away down a stormwater drain or by a gush of water. Or your baby or child drowns in a pool, or in the sea.

It's a dream people are often too frightened to mention, because they fear the dream is precognitive—a glimpse of the future. They somehow believe that talking about the dream will make it even more likely to happen, so they keep it to themselves. And they're scared. So if you've had this dream and think you're on your own, think again. Ask around. Do a survey. You'll find many parents who recall dreams easily have had this dream, or variations of it.

The first tip is to share your dream with other parents so they can free themselves from living in fear, believing they will lose their child. What a relief to discover you've had a very common, symbolic dream! So, what does it mean?

You must have noticed the connecting factor—water. Water in dreams often represents your emotions.

Parenthood is an extremely emotional time. It would be easy to say this dream comes up because parents worry about protecting their children from danger. But dreams go deeper than that, and dreams are more about YOU than about other people. The baby or child in your dream may look like your son or daughter, but really is a symbol of something in danger of 'disappearing down the plughole' or getting washed away and lost in your own life. Think, "Don't throw the baby out with the bathwater!"

to begin to get some insight here. For new parents, especially stay-at-home parents, there is so much change occurring at this time. What hopes, dreams, needs, or lifestyles seem to be slipping away, when you have this dream?

Also see Tips 27, 46, 59

Don't throw the baby out with the bathwater

Tip 41
If you fall in a dream will you die in your sleep?

How many times have you woken up on the brink of death, perhaps falling a long way, the ground rushing up at you, or having the cold metal of a gun pressed to your forehead and hearing the trigger being pulled, or being unable to breathe, aware of suffocating?

And how many times have you been frightened to go back to sleep, that night or for weeks to come, in case the dream returns? How much of that fear is fuelled by the story you've heard that if you die in your dream, you'll die in your sleep?

People do die in their sleep, but no one has ever been able to ask if they were dreaming at the time! Rest assured, though, that the old wives' tale is not true. It's quite common to have a dream where you experience death and then move on to the next part of your dream, still very much alive. Oh, and you also get to wake up in the morning!

If you don't wake up during a falling dream, there are two common dream outcomes. In one version, you have a surprisingly soft landing and walk away unharmed. In the other version you die, but then find yourself looking at your dead body before moving on to the next part of your dream. The same two options usually come up for other dreams where you dream you are about to die.

These dreams are symbolic. They come up when you are on the brink of drastic change within yourself, or in your life circumstances. Your dreaming mind sees the 'old you' dying off and the 'new you' emerging. A soft landing dream suggests you are handling the transition smoothly. The version where you see yourself dead suggests a deeper change, and a readiness to face and grieve the passing of the 'old you' combined with a welcoming of the new.

When you dream you see yourself in a coffin, ask what form you are in as observer. If you are in physical form, like an onlooker, then you are simply facing the death of the 'old you', and all the feelings that go along with that as you farewell one stage of your life and move forward with the changes. If you dream you are in spirit form, or feel you are invisible, your dream suggests you are finding it difficult to let go of the 'old you' and find a suitable 'new you' approach to life. It's time to grieve the past, let go, and flow with new opportunities.

Let old attitudes fall away

Tip 42
Too gruesome …

ave you ever held back from sharing a dream because it was so gruesome and sickening? Have you ever wondered what your dreams really say about your sanity? You may wake up feeling your usual, balanced self, but why have you spent a night dreaming about lopping off people's heads, or wading through dismembered bodies, blood, and guts? Are you harbouring unconscious masochistic or murderous tendencies, or are you on the edge of a descent into madness? Can there be anything uplifting and positive about these dreams, any nuggets of gold you can gather from the battlefields of the night?

Most people experience such gruesome dreams from time to time. These dreams are healthy and normal, and can be very insightful and helpful when you interpret them.

The first tip is not to focus on the horror, but to take a huge step back and look at the big picture presented by dismembered bodies, wounds, cuts, and bruises. The big picture here is that something that should be whole (a body), is not, and the reason it is not whole is that it has been wounded or hurt in some way.

Turn this big picture summary into a question and ask, "Where in my life today do I feel wounded, hurt, and incomplete (not whole) or disconnected (lopped off)?"

Each part of the body has a function: legs for movement, arms for embracing, hands for doing, head for thinking, eyes for seeing, and so on. Which body parts are hurt, missing, or feeling disconnected in your dream? No hands? What is crippling your ability to do and handle things? No head? What is stopping you from thinking about things? No heart? What has hurt you so badly to make you disconnect from your feelings?

Dismembered dreams help you to see where you are not fully functioning at present. They help you to acknowledge your emotional wounds, and to see how these have affected you. They help you to see which hurts you need to heal to become whole.

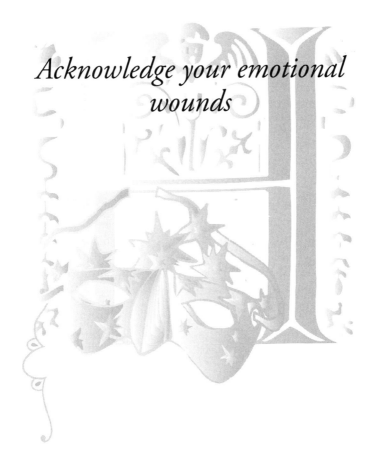

Acknowledge your emotional wounds

5

People in dreams

Tip 43
What you did in my dream last night

What do you think of me, the author of this book? It's a serious question! You've come to know me a little through these tips. How would you describe my personality? Write your answers down. Now, imagine the answers other readers have given. Do you think they might have picked similar descriptions to yours? The chances are that there will be a variety of responses, because we all see people through different eyes, according to our individual experiences.

If you're not convinced, try this experiment. Sit down with three friends, and together write a list of five people you all know, and then five well-known people familiar to you all. Then each take a piece of paper, and write down three words describing the personality of each of these ten people. For example, you might describe one person as 'shy, deep thinker, resentful'. Compare notes. How different were your responses?

We don't really know other people as they truly are. We see them through the veil of our own life experiences. In this way, how we describe other people tells us more about who we are than who they are.

It's the same in dreams. When you dream of other people, it's usually because your dreaming mind has chosen these people to represent the qualities you see in them. You might dream of someone you see as shy when your dream is exploring either your own shyness or—as is often the case—the opposite, your confidence.

People in your dreams are symbols. Psychic connections in a dream are extremely rare. How someone treats you in a dream is a product of your dreaming mind. No matter how real the dream seems, always remember that people in your dreams represent your own beliefs and feelings, not theirs. So rather than be hurt or upset by another person's actions in your dreams, ask what you can learn about yourself from the way your dreaming mind presents this person. Self-knowledge is power.

Also see Tip 76

How you see someone reveals something about you

Tip 44
Sex with someone you shouldn't have

ave you ever turned up at work, looked a colleague in the eye, and suddenly remembered a dream you had last night? You know, the dream where you two were having sex and ... mortified you avert your eyes, blush, stutter, wonder if it was a shared dream, a deeply buried fantasy, or a telepathic desire beamed out by your colleague while you slept.

Admit it. Everyone, absolutely everyone, has had, and will have, this kind of dream. It's normal and natural, and the only reason we think it's not is that everyone's too embarrassed to talk about it.

It's also 100% symbolic, so don't follow through with 'I had a precognitive dream about you last night' or treat the poor, unsuspecting, innocent colleague with disgust.

It's all about you! Sex in dreams is about what qualities or attitudes you are integrating into your life, as sex is a brilliant symbol of integration where two bodies become one. Ask what three words best describe your dream lover's personality or approach to life. These are the qualities your dream is integrating into your being. Good sex: good integration. Bad sex: warning, think again about your new approach.

Also see Tips 43, 49, 80

Describe your dream lover's personality in three words

Tip 45
Cheating partner

When you dream about your partner cheating on you, is your dream giving you a hint that all is not well in your relationship? Should you hire a private detective, confront your partner, or give the cold shoulder?

You could ask a similar question when you dream your six-month old baby is chatting in adult language to the cat: is your dream giving you a hint that your child is a genius? Or if you dream your deceased grandmother is alive and well and having an affair with your local baker, should you rewrite the family history? Clearly not. As you can see, the dreams of your baby and deceased grandmother are obviously symbolic, and the truth is that your cheating dream is too. Confusion arises with cheating dreams because the subject is so emotive, and these dreams always seem so real. Your partner looks like your partner, the dream scenario is usually quite logical, and the feelings of betrayal and distress are immense.

This is a very common dream, and many an innocent partner has been on the receiving end of short shrift the next day, totally unaware and confused about why their partner is treating them so meanly.

In rare cases, your dream might have some accuracy as your unconscious mind puts two-and-two together while you sleep and comes up with four, but please remember that the dreaming mind is far more obscure. In fact, if your partner was cheating on you, a dream containing this information is more likely to present in a more symbolic form.

So, you and millions of other people with faithful partners have this dream and want to know why and what to do about it. Here's how to approach any dream about your partner, whether the dream action is cheating or anything else.

Regard your partner in a dream as symbolic, not real. He or she may seem to be your partner, but just like any other person, animal, thing, or place in a dream, your partner represents something about you. Sometimes your partner represents your beliefs and feelings about your relationship, and sometimes your beliefs and feelings about how you relate to the world in general, but the dream is never about your partner. For partner dreams, ask how you feel in the dream. In the common cheating dream, you feel cheated or betrayed. Ask where in your life today you feel cheated and betrayed, or where you might be cheating or betraying your own best interests. Is it you who is cheating—not on your partner—but cheating yourself out of a getting the best deal in life? What can you do to make this right, to be faithful to your best interests?

Also see Tip 43

Tip 46
Dream babies and children

ream babies or children provide strong clues to interpreting the dreams in which they appear. Are you ready to play detective? This is what to do.

Firstly, ask, "How old is the child?" Don't fight any logic, just quickly name the age of the baby or child. You'll be surprised how quickly you answer. A certain age will just feel right.

Imagine you said, "Six months old." In this example, your dream is about something that's been in your life for six months. This may sound far too simple to be true, yet it is one of the most accurate indicators of the subject matter of a dream. Why is this?

Imagine beginning a new job or relationship. Your mind records this event as the introduction of something new into your life, a new beginning, the birth of a new period of your life. Your dreaming mind thinks largely in pictures, and so it will often picture that event as a new baby. Now imagine, six months later, an issue coming up around that relationship or job. Your dreaming mind conjures up the perfect symbol—a six-month-old baby to match the age of the job or relationship in question.

People are always so surprised that dreams, which seem to be so illogical and timeless, actually have a precise grip on time. You'll often dream about issues on their anniversaries, long after you've forgotten the details. For example, you might not remember that you went into hospital for a painful operation on March 6 many years ago, but your dreams will often revisit any lingering issues around that experience on March 6 for years to come, until you heal them.

So, back to those dream babies and children. You now have a figure, let's say, 'eight-years-old'. Next, ask, "What has been in my life for eight years?" You might answer, "My current relationship is eight-years-old."

Then ask what happened to the baby or child in your dream. For example, you might say, "The child was hurt, and I was trying to comfort her."

Finally, ask how this applies to your eight-year relationship. You'll be surprised how quickly you see the parallel between the two. In this example, you might relate to a feeling of hurt in your relationship, a hurt you may have overlooked, a hurt that needs addressing.

Play detective

Tip 47
Messages from the other side

When someone who has died appears to you in a dream, are they communicating with you from the afterlife, or are these dreams symbolic? Dreaming of a loved one after death can be the most precious, comforting, uplifting experience, especially when the dream is full of love, embraces, and tender messages, and when the person looks healthy, full of life, and perhaps even presents at a different age—younger for someone who died in old age, adult for a child who died young.

Many a bereaved dreamer cherishes such exquisite moments in a dream, and although they wake up to a world empty of their loved one, they draw strength from the night-time encounter and a feeling of support to get through the early days.

Many more wish they could have just one such dream, and often feel devastated and abandoned when they discover that their loved one is appearing in other people's dreams, but not in their own.

On the other hand, many bereaved people have experienced distressing dreams where the deceased person, loving and kind in life, is completely different in dreams—angry, blaming, hurtful, controlling, or condemning. In other cases, people who were difficult in life continue to be difficult in dreams, often leaving dreamers feeling the deceased person is controlling them and restraining them from moving on with life.

There are instances where accurate information has been communicated by the deceased in dreams; information, for example, about the circumstances of death, that have been later verified. However, these are extremely rare. Contact through dreams in the early days following death may sometimes be the case, but as time passes, you can be increasingly certain that these dreams are symbolic. If a loving person acts negatively in a dream, you can be certain your dream is symbolic.

Dreams of the deceased usually deal with grief and healing. For example, it is normal, during grieving, to feel angry with the person for dying and abandoning you, even though this is irrational. When anger, abandonment and blame come up in your dreams, these are your own emotions being processed. When forgiveness and letting go come up in these dreams, these reflect your own readiness to heal and move on, your own resting in peace.

Look at the person appearing in your dream as symbolising your loss, or your feelings about death, or your feelings about that person and the role they played in your life, and then see the rest of the dream as exploring and resolving these issues within yourself.

Tip 48
Parents and guardians

I f you could make a list of all the people who have appeared in your dreams, who would come out top? The chances are it would be one or both of your parents—or whoever was mainly responsible for your upbringing as a child.

From babyhood, you learned to see the world through the eyes of your guardians or parents. They were your role models. You learned habits, attitudes, responses, and reactions to the world from them. They taught you what they believed to be right and wrong. From your very first days, your mother taught you what a mother is, what a mother does, and what to expect from a mother. Your father taught you what a father is, what a father does, and what to expect from a father. You learned mothering and fathering from your guardians.

Well, you know what happened in the next phase of your life, those teenage years! You began to question everything you had learned from your guardians. This important, normal and natural period was all about becoming an individual. Your guardians had kept you safe and helped you to grow to a stage where you could have your own experiences, make sense of the changing world, and find your place as a unique adult. All those habits, attitudes, responses, and reactions to the world you had learned from them were under fire.

But old habits die hard. Most of the attitudes you learned from your parents were rock solid, there to stay, whether or not they were appropriate for you as an adult. You were happy with some. They felt good and right. You were very unhappy with some, and, as a natural result, you took a complete opposite stance: for example, where they believed in rules, you believed in freedom, or perhaps where they believed in holding your tongue, you believed in speaking up.

If you could examine all your attitudes and beliefs, you'd find that most stem back to those early lessons from your parents. Most are either the same as, or in direct opposition to, those of your parents. In an ideal world, you would do best to walk a compassionate middle path (Chinese Buddhists might call this the Tao) between these extremes, a path from which you could understand all points of view.

When you dream of your mother, father, or guardian, you are most likely dreaming about the attitudes and beliefs you learned from them, especially those that are relevant to your current situation. When your parents appear in your dreams, ask how much you are like or unlike them, and how much this is affecting the way you approach your life today. Which attitudes do you need to change for a better outcome?

Tip 49
Ex-partners

Just how many times do ex-partners need to keep popping up in your dreams? You've said goodbye, moved on, found your 'happily-ever-after', and rarely think about this ex until he makes his appearance in your dreams.

Or is your situation different? Do you wish he were not so ex, and wonder if your dreams signal you should make a move to reignite the old flame?

In dreams you may find yourself attracted to an ex physically, perhaps having sex; emotionally, perhaps feeling a special bond; mentally, perhaps enjoying a joke; or spiritually, perhaps feeling forgiveness or unconditional love. On the other hand, these dreams may be full of anger, blame, and guilt. Your waking feelings may be positive or negative, and your current partner may be distressed—even jealous—to hear of these dreams. How should you interpret them?

To state the obvious, relationships have a huge impact on you. When you look back on your life, you probably measure it out as much in relationships as any other indicator. You associate times in your life with different partners. Your relationships influence your attitudes and highlight your sensitivities. And when relationships end, they often do so with unresolved issues hanging in the air.

When you dream of an ex, it is usually because those issues, attitudes, and sensitivities have been triggered in the last two days, either by your current relationship or by other circumstances.

When the dreams are loving and kind, you are resolving your own past hurts, understanding the relationship in hindsight, feeling forgiveness for yourself and for the ex, or simply noting those qualities you admired in your ex-partner or enjoyed in your life back then that you'd like to introduce into your current life. In less uplifting dreams, you may find yourself getting back in touch with feelings you repressed during the relationship: anger, blame, guilt or grief, for example.

Either way these dreams are opportunities to revisit the past, to learn, and to heal, so that you can apply new wisdom to your current circumstance and move forward. Assure your present partner that far from these dreams being about any hidden desire to hook up with an ex, they're all about freeing yourself from emotional baggage and making peace with your past.

Also see Tips 43, 78

Make peace with your past

Tip 50
Finding your soul mate in a dream

Have you met your soul mate in your dreams? Perhaps you have glimpsed your soul mate on the horizon, heard his voice, felt his presence. Or maybe you have been magnetically drawn to look deeply into his eyes, seeing perfect love within. Or felt his unwavering support, his total commitment to you, his ability to help you along your way, knowing exactly what you need. Or felt his embrace—protective, lingering, heart-tripping, a promise or fulfilment of passionately loving sex.

Have you woken up wishing you could capture the details of his face, or with his features firmly etched into your heart? Have you wondered how to find him, where to begin your search to find the man—or woman—of your dreams?

This experience is so warm, real, and uplifting that many a dreamer has spurned other lovers and endlessly searched: for the search is endless. The dream soul mate does not exist—except deep within your own soul.

This dream comes up when it's time for you to connect with all those wonderful qualities you sensed in your dream soul mate—to find and connect with these qualities within you. They are there! You wouldn't have felt them in your dream if they were not! It's time for you to bring these qualities up from where they are hiding or latent in your unconscious, and introduce them to the light of day.

Dreams love to play with words. When you look deeply into your dream lover's eyes, you are looking—and feeling—deeply into your own 'I'. You are 'I to I' or face to face with yourself. Well, not face to face perhaps, but soul to soul, through your eyes, the windows of the soul.

Name the three top qualities you admired or longed for in your dream soul mate, the qualities that warmed and completed you. These are the qualities you need to locate within yourself, and nourish and encourage into your everyday being. Here's the best secret of all. When you connect with your inner soul mate, your perfect partner usually appears in your life, attracted by ... his soul mate, you.

Have you wondered how to find him?

Tip 51
Character actors and bit roles

re your dreams populated by people from fairytales and legends? Do you meet kings, queens, witches, heroes, prostitutes, priests, saboteurs, wise women, paupers, saints, addicts, presidents, Cinderellas, angels, rescuers, lawyers, orphans, clowns, healers, revolutionaries, enemies, police, martyrs, nurses, victims, innocents, servants or masters? The cast is much greater than those mentioned here, but you'll know them when you meet them.

Whenever these people—or any other characters or role players —appear in your dreams, they represent energies influencing your life today. Sounds spooky? No, it's not like that. These aren't disembodied energies floating in and out of your dreams, guiding or misguiding you throughout your days. These are your own energies, related to your beliefs about life. Here's how it works.

If you dream about a prostitute, ask where in your life today you might be prostituting yourself, not sexually, but perhaps selling your soul for money, 'selling out' or selling yourself short, or responding to this kind of energy around you.

If you dream about a hero, ask where, in your life today, you are acting the hero, or responding to hero energies around you. In the case of a dream Cinderella, ask where in your life today you feel like Cinderella, or you feel as if you are dealing with a Cinderella kind of person.

Meet a dream nurse? Ask yourself what healing or nursing energies are in your life. Sense a saboteur lurking in the background? Quick, identify him and smoke him out! Ask yourself in what way you might be sabotaging your plans and wishes, or where this energy is playing out in your life today.

Get the picture? These dream characters, or archetypes as they are often referred to in dreams, stories, and movies, summarise the kinds of energies we all meet or express at certain times in our lives. Your dream dramas reveal the interplay of these energies in your life today, helping you to see what is working for you and what is working against you.

When you have a dream featuring one or more of these characters, imagine that your life is a fairytale and you are its author. How would you change the storyline for the best outcome? Rewrite your dream in its new happily-ever-after form, making sure all actions are loving actions. How can you translate this formula into your daily life, to create a brilliant outcome?

Imagine your life is a fairytale and you are its author

Tip 52
Checklist

People are such perfect dream symbols for your various beliefs, issues, thoughts, feelings, attitudes, memories, and experiences, but sometimes you need a little extra help narrowing the field when interpreting the meaning of a certain person in a particular dream.

After reading the other dream tips in this section, use this checklist to search for other possible meanings for a person appearing in a dream.

What is the personality of this person (three words or phrases)?
How does this person approach life (three words or phrases)?
When was the last time you saw, heard of or interacted with this person?
What were the circumstances of your answer to the last question?
How would you feel if you met this person today?
Who else does this person remind you of?
Is there a pun or different meaning in this person's name?
What role does this person play in the world?
What role does this person play in your life?
Which three things do you admire about this person?
Which three things do you dislike about this person (be honest)?
Do you have any unresolved feelings or business with this person?
If so, what?
What belief might you have borrowed from this person?
Do you need to make peace with this person?
If you were to meet this person today, what message would you like to deliver?

(This checklist is extracted from *Dream Alchemy*, by Jane Teresa Anderson, published by Hachette Livre.)

If you met this person today, what message would you like to deliver?

6

Emotions and feelings in dreams

Tip 53
Mood paintings

reams are the result of your mind processing your experiences of the last 24–48 hours, updating your view of the world and how you see yourself fitting into it. The language may seem weird, but then what else can you expect when your logical brain is taking a rest? Your thinking cap switches off when you dream, leaving your creative, inventive, expressive self free to come out and play, to paint your feelings as dreams.

Look at your dreams through the eyes of a playful child, a child who doesn't speak your everyday language but who expresses mood and ideas in her own way. What is your dream child expressing in your dream about the real mood of your last two days?

To get 100% from life,
get 100% from sleep!

Deep regenerative sleep is vital for healing your organs and mind as well as regulating energy production and your immune system. You can dramatically improve your sleep quality by making adjustments to very basic routines and to your sleep environment.

Some Benefits of a Healthy Sleep

1. Essential for healing and restoration of the body
2. Promotes a healthier heart
3. Enhances mood and general feeling of well-being
4. Improves alertness and concentration
5. May assist in losing weight and making you look younger
6. Reduces the risk of depression
7. Improves memory
8. Reduces inflammation
9. Decreases stress
10. Boosts your immune system

For further information, or to arrange an <u>obligation free</u> Healthy Sleep System consultation freecall 1800 006 606 (Australia) or 0800 006 606 (New Zealand). Alternatively, please visit: <u>dreamtip102.wenatex.com.au</u>

When calling, please be sure to <u>mention this book</u>.

Pedimol
Traditional Herbal Cream

MADE IN AUSTRIA FOR OVER 60 YEARS

Pedimol Herbal Cream contains a traditional German herbal formula that has been handed down for generations. It is a highly effective, cooling, anti-inflammatory, pain relieving, joint and muscle liniment that brings notable results.

The genuine soothing herbal cream can be used on the hands, feet, arms, legs, or the body after a bath. It is also ideal for relaxing massage, sport massage and reflex massage.

Special Offer!

Order three tubes of Pedimol to receive a bulk order discount!

☐ Single 50ml Tube $19.95

☐ Three 50ml Tubes $52.50

Freecall Wenatex on: 1800 006 606 (Australia) or 0800 006 606 (New Zealand) today!

When calling, please be sure to <u>mention this book</u>.

wenatex
The Sleep System

www.wenatex.com.au
www.wenatex.co.nz

You paint your feelings as dreams

Tip 54
Anger and rage

When did you last feel angry in a dream? How did you express it: a tight-lipped suppression, a brooding sulk, a breathy curse? Did you give the finger, kick the cat, or throw a tantrum? Or did you explode into rage overdrive, screaming self-righteously at the offending person, or picking them up and throwing them repeatedly against a wall until they were as floppy as a rag doll? Shocking? Yes, and no. This is a very common and extremely healthy dream, though it is not one many people will admit to having.

Think about this. How do you feel when you wake up from a rage dream? How do you feel as the day progresses? At first your dream verbal abuse or violence may shock you, but as the day unfolds, you usually notice a deep sense of calm. Looking back on your dream, you may rightly conclude that a good deal of anger was safely released, with no one being hurt, but you might be completely baffled as to why you were angry in the first place, and why you were angry with this particular dream character.

While your anger or rage dream acts as a safety valve to keep you sane, it's important to understand that you are having this dream because you are bottling up feelings of anger in your life and this is unhealthy for you in the long run. Repressed anger is believed to contribute to serious diseases such as cancer, stroke, or heart attack. Anger is never the real issue. It's what you feel angry about that is the real issue, the thing you need to face and address in your life.

Your anger dream will be full of clues about the real issue, so use those dream interpretation skills you're gathering from this book to identify that issue, and resolve it once and for all.

*Anger is the smokescreen hiding
the burning issue*

Tip 55
Crying and grief

When you wake up crying real tears, or simply feeling profoundly sad for no apparent reason, it's because you have finally touched upon some buried grief through a dream. You may have released it all, or there may be more to come. Either way, this is good and healing. (Don't you always feel much better after a cry?) Even if you don't remember the dream, rest assured that tears are better out than in, and although you may become more aware in the next few days of a past event that caused you grief, you are well on the way to finally letting it go and moving on.

There will be times in your past where you were unable to express your grief, or where you felt you should try to hide it. Perhaps 'boys don't cry', or you were advised to 'keep a stiff upper lip', or you accepted a hurtful situation as normal or something to be endured, so you packed grief away, out of sight. Or perhaps the only way to get through a situation was to pretend to yourself that it wasn't happening, or wasn't important, or that you were coping wonderfully, or needed to smile for others, or that you had already healed.

These, and other forms of denial, are like bandaids. They work on the surface, but the deeper wound still hurts, affecting how you live your life. One day the grief finally breaks through—perhaps accompanied by a dream of a dam bursting, or a tsunami breaking—and you wake up crying.

If you can remember your dream, look for clues about your grief; understanding the past will help you to accelerate your healing. Look for a young child or younger person who seems sad, or hurt, or trying to cover up his or her feelings. What age is the child? Ask what happened for you at that age, or that number of years ago. It doesn't matter whether the child or person looks like you. He or she most likely symbolises the event or your hurt.

Also look for historical markers in your dream: perhaps cars, houses, clothes, or numbers that help to give you a time period to explore.

When you have found the source of your grief, do this dream alchemy practice. Close your eyes, and visualise hugging and comforting yourself as you were back then, or hugging and comforting the child in the dream. Let her cry all her tears dry, then let her smile and laugh and grow strong and happy. Tell her how wonderful her life will be now that her tears have washed it all away, and see her growing before your eyes, changing and becoming a strong, happy, powerful, and relieved new you. Merge with her in your mind's eye, and take her, fully healed, into your heart.

When you cry away grief, rainbows appear

Tip 56
Pain and hurt

Have you ever felt physical pain in a dream? Perhaps you've felt a snake bite, or a blow to your head, or a piece of flesh ripped out in an accident. Have you felt emotional pain in a dream—betrayal, heartbreak, anguish, abandonment, regret, guilt, shock, devastation?

When you feel physical or emotional pain in a dream, it usually relates to an emotional hurt you are carrying. Your dream might be expressing a hurt feeling from the last day or two. This is a healthy way to process and release the pain. However it might be referencing a hurt from your past, one that has taken a deep hold, or one that you have buried in your unconscious. Wouldn't it be wonderful if you could deal with painful experiences by just digging a hole and burying them? Unfortunately, it doesn't work that way. Your unconscious mind is so powerful that it affects the way you see and respond to the world. For example, you may have forgotten how hurt you felt when your best friend betrayed you, but have you noticed that you seem to have a natural distrust for anyone who reminds you of her? Or you may have forgotten how abandoned you felt when your twin sisters were born and you were sent to live with an aunt for a month while your mother recovered, but have you noticed how clingy you are in your relationships?

When you feel pain in a dream, ask what emotional hurt you are experiencing today. If nothing relates, consider this an old emotional injury that is crying out for you to address, or that is in the process of finally being acknowledged and released. The symbols in your dream will help you identify that past hurt. Look for dream clues to pinpoint the time of the hurt, clues such as people you knew back then, fashions, houses you once lived in.

If a past hurt is still an extremely sensitive issue, it might appear in your dream as an animal or child in physical or emotional distress. The sad, abandoned child might be expressing your hurt feelings of abandonment, (though she may also represent something you have abandoned), and that loyal little puppy with its heart exposed and bleeding might represent your hurt feelings of betrayal (though he may also represent something you have betrayed).

Celebrate any dream that reveals pain or hurt, because it is an opportunity to acknowledge and release your hurt from its hiding place, and to heal and move on. Do this simply by closing your eyes and visualising healing the dream hurt in this way. Hug the abandoned child, and make her feel wanted and loved, or wave a magic wand over the puppy's heart to stop it bleeding and then tuck it back into place and seal the wound. When you do this dream alchemy practice, your unconscious mind follows this cue, reversing the damage and any inappropriate beliefs you picked up as a result of the original trauma.

Tip 57
An emotional barometer

ow are you feeling right now? Answer before reading on. Give three different words to describe how you are feeling right now.

If you find it difficult to tune into your emotions and feelings by day, look to your dreams for clues, because it's those feelings and emotions you can't name that may be blocking your way forward in life. Your dreams show you how your emotions and feelings are working for or against you, whether or not you are aware of them when your eyes are open.

One place to start is the weather in your dreams. Think of your dream weather as a barometer of your feelings. Your dreaming mind often uses weather in this way because it is such a perfect metaphor, one we use in everyday conversation: "She's got a sunny disposition" (happy, optimistic), "He lives under a black cloud" (pessimistic, in a black mood), "She stormed out" (angry), "He's a breath of fresh air" (refreshed, uplifted), "I woke up in a fog" (unclear), "She's icy" (frozen or uncaring).

Here are some suggestions for interpreting your feelings according to dream weather symbols. Rainbow: hopeful. Light rain: refreshed or cleansed. Heavy rain: sad, teary. Black clouds: angry. Bolt of lightning: shocked, enlightened, inspired. Snowy: snowed-under. Flood: flooded, deluged, overwhelmed. Stifling heat: stifled, suffocated. Frost: frosty. Ice: cold, unsafe. Sunny: happy, relaxed. Very sunny: burnt, uncomfortable. Bright: uplifted, clever, optimistic. Humid: hot under the collar, embarrassed. Windy: changeable, choppy, unsettled. Tornado: fearful, frenzied, calm in the centre.

Remember, though, these are only suggestions to demonstrate the way it works. The bottom line when it comes to interpreting any dream symbol rests with you. If you find thunderstorms exciting, then your dream thunderstorms may symbolise excitement; someone else may find thunderstorms threatening, so their dream thunderstorms might symbolise feeling threatened.

Look at the weather in your dreams, and ask, "What in my life is like a thunderstorm/ rain cloud/ rainbow/ snowstorm/ gale force wind …?" Your answer will help you get in touch with your feelings about that situation. What can you do in your life to change your emotional weather? Cry away a black cloud? Find hope by bringing on a rainbow after the rain? Melt ice by letting someone get close? Find a way to follow these where you can, and watch the sun rise again.

Where is the impending storm in your life?

Tip 58
When one thing leads to another

Imagine that both Tom and Andrew had the same dream. Each dreamed he was on his way to the airport to fly to another city for a work meeting when he realised he had left his ticket at home. He wondered whether he had time to go back home and get his ticket, or whether he would miss the plane. The dream ended there. What does it mean?

The in-depth interpretation depends on how Tom and Andrew each felt in their dream, and this applies to most dream interpretations.

Tom felt panicked by the delay, and then excited by the challenge. The adrenalin rush of racing back home to get the ticket in time to catch the plane would put him on a high that would energise him right through the meeting, and impress his work colleagues with his 'can do', risk-taking, adventurous approach.

Andrew felt immediately relieved. He was off the hook with a perfect excuse. Forgetting his ticket meant he didn't have to face his colleagues. He fleetingly wondered whether he had forgotten his ticket accidentally-on-purpose, but dismissed the thought as soon as he realised he could now spend the afternoon relaxing and playing golf.

Tom and Andrew's dreams were about why they have been experiencing delays in achieving their goals. Both dreams reveal a saboteur element: both Tom and Andrew are creating the very delays that daily despair them. "Why," they each moan, "does life keep blocking me?"

As you can see by examining their dream feelings, Tom loves the thrill of an obstacle course and believes the challenge of the added difficulties gives him a performance edge and wins him praise. He unconsciously creates delays to experience a high because he believes he needs the rush to perform, and craves praise for achieving against the odds.

Andrew, on the other hand, fears achieving his goals or facing up to his abilities, whether or not he's equal to the task. He unconsciously creates delays to safeguard him from this pressure, though he won't admit this to anyone—including himself—in daily life. Sometimes he catches a glimpse of his modus operandi, but then swings denial into place deftly with his golf clubs.

Here's the tip. When you write out a dream, add your feelings. Make sure you don't write about how you would feel if this happened to you in waking life. Write the feelings you felt while you were in the dream. Then highlight the feeling words, and link them together in the same order to form a flow. For example, Tom's would read: panicked -> excited -> high -> energised -> impressive -> risky -> adventurous. Andrew's would read: relieved-> excused-> dismissive-> relaxed.

Do this for your dreams, and ask where this pattern is playing out in your life. You will see your life in quite a different light. Once you are aware of this pattern, you have the power to change it into one that brings you greater rewards.

7

Dream settings

Tip 59
Water and seascapes

How many of your dream settings involve water? Do you find yourself on the shore, sailing the ocean, swimming in the sea or in swimming pools, escaping leaking flooding buildings, navigating rivers, drowning in murky water, breathing underwater, finding your road blocked by floods, being stranded by tides, or wondering if a dam is going to burst?

Watery dreams usually represent your emotions. Overwhelming waves of emotion often show up as tsunamis in dreams, and you can read more about those in Tip 22. It makes sense that we all tend to dream watery symbols for our emotions. We describe water in emotional terms—a raging torrent, a calm lake, a stagnant pool. Emotions and water flow. They come in waves. They can be deep or shallow. They can be supportive, or we can find ourselves out of our depth in them.

Our emotions can be crystal clear, or murky and shark-infested. They can leave us stranded as they ebb and flow, leaving us joyful one moment, depressed the next. They can flood us when we least expect them, and they can powerfully block our progress. We can feel as if we're drowning in emotions, or we can suddenly discover how to flow with an emotion, how to handle or navigate it, perhaps even how to draw sustenance from it, to breathe underwater. We can dam up our emotions—but only for a limited time before they burst through.

Look at the water in your dream, and ask what emotion or feeling it seems to portray, guided by the examples given here. As dreams are the battleground of many emotional issues, are you really surprised to encounter so many watery dream scenes?

The dream ocean can also represent your unconscious mind, in contrast to the firm and shore (sure?) land that often symbolises your conscious mind. The land is knowable. You can see it, touch it, and feel it. The ocean is a great and deep mystery, like your unconscious mind, but you can dip into it in dreams. Lurking beneath its surface are your fears dressed as sharks, and your miraculous, undiscovered genius dressed as awesome whales. Welcome your watery dreams, and explore.

Also see Tip 22

Are your emotions crystal clear, murky or shark infested?

Tip 60
Landscapes

How many different landscapes have you encountered in your dreams? Have you visited mountains, forests, deserts, foreign cities, unknown suburbs, rolling hills and valleys, lush countryside, steep rock cliffs, or barren wastelands? What do these dream settings mean?

The landscape in your dream helps describe the situation you find yourself in, the one your dream sets out to explore.

If you find yourself in a dream desert, for example, you might be dreaming about a situation in your life today where you are feeling isolated, or deserted, or where you are feeling a bit dry emotionally. What happens in your dream desert represents your feelings about this, as well as possible solutions to your situation.

If your dream setting is a rocky, mountainous region with no easy road through, you might be dreaming about a situation in your life today where the challenges seem insurmountable, with no easy way through.

Or perhaps you find yourself in a foreign city, one you haven't visited before, among people who speak a language you do not know. In this case, you might be dreaming about a situation in your life today where you feel as if you are in foreign territory, perhaps beginning a new university course, or finding yourself in different social circles amidst different attitudes.

Applying the same approach, you may find yourself in lush countryside when you are dreaming about a situation in your life today where opportunities are growing fast, or you may find yourself in a concrete, industrial suburb when you are dreaming about a situation where you feel hard work is dominating natural pleasures.

In dreams featuring landscapes, ask which situation in your life today feels like the dream setting. Once you've identified the situation, you can interpret the rest of your dream, confident of the subject matter it is exploring.

What feels like a desert in your life?

Tip 61
Travel and transport

How many of your dream settings are journeys? Whether you're travelling by foot, car, horse, train, bus, plane, hot air balloon, or a fabulous futuristic vehicle, your journey dreams are about how you're progressing in the various journeys of your life. There's your spiritual journey from birth to death; your career journey up or down corporate ladders, in and out of jobs; your relationship journey from initial attraction to wherever it goes … and so on.

In any journey there are ups and downs, obstacles, dramas, moments of insight that catapult you leaps and bounds ahead, moments of doubt that grind you to a halt. There are times when you sail forth at great speed when your dreams might see you enjoying a gust of wind carrying you along in your dream yacht.

There are times when your journey takes you along well-defined, disciplined routes with no leeway for leaving the designated track, such as when you're studying for a degree or undergoing a strict training, and your dreams might see you travelling by train on rigid tracks.

And there are times when you might be flying high, with or without the help of a plane in your dreams. When you ride with your passions, you might dream travel by horse, and when you need to slow down and rest, your dream car might spring a flat tyre. You get the picture.

Travelling by cycle in a dream might remind you that some of life's journeys are cycles: the cycles relationships go through, the cycles of birth and death you meet along your spiritual journey, the ebbs and flows that come and go as surely as the tides and the seasons.

If you run a one-person business, you may often dream travel on a cycle, a one-person mode of transport where you have to do all the hard work by yourself with no engine to help you.

If your dream vehicle is futuristic, it may symbolise your totally innovative approach to achieving your goal, or new ways of approaching life that are still forming within your mind's eye, more in the future than in the present.

Ideally, life is about moving forward on all fronts, although there are times when you may feel you're falling behind or going backwards, only to later discover that these reversals led you to a better place. Interpret your dream journeys for maximum insight into how you're faring, and hunt for dream clues to open your eyes to possible alternative paths.

Also see Tips 29, 30, 97

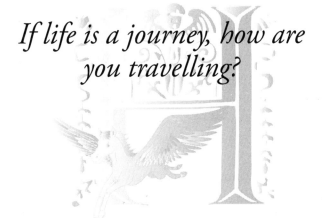

If life is a journey, how are you travelling?

Tip 62
Houses and buildings

ouse hunting again? Do you spend dreams looking for a new place to live, or a great place to renovate? Or do you find yourself in a share house, mansion, rundown shack, penthouse, university department, or castle? Are your dream buildings new, falling apart, or missing important rooms?

You have to hand it to your dreams, cleverly creating architectural designs, interior décor and original furnishings from the recesses of your unconscious mind. Many a good creative idea produced by a dream has been put into production in waking life. But when it comes to dream interpretation, what do your dream buildings, rooms and furnishings mean?

Dream houses and other buildings usually represent you—your body, mind, and soul. Houses and buildings are for living and working in, and this is one reason why your dreams often use them as symbols of you, as they arc the 'building' you live and work in, the architecture of your mind and being.

When you're exploring new ways of being, you'll often find yourself searching for a new home in a dream. You'll consider dream renovating a tumbledown home when you've been feeling run down and you're ready to renew and perhaps expand your thinking and being. You'll dream of house hunting when you're changing how you express yourself in life, looking for a dream building that expresses the new you.

A spacious dream home with amazing views might parallel the way you are expanding your mind and discovering new and amazing ways to view life. A dream castle might mirror feelings of grandeur, or a defensive attitude.

The key to interpreting a building in a dream is to describe its personality. What is the personality of an English Victorian manor house? Imposing? Strict? Imperial? What is the personality of a beach shack? Carefree? Unmotivated? Falling apart? Your dreaming mind created your dream building, so it's how you see the personality of the place that reveals what it symbolises about you.

Also see Tip 24

Every dream building has character

Tip 63
Off the planet, UFOs and aliens

ave you ever seen a UFO or an alien in your dreams? Have you communicated with extraterrestrials, or visited other planets? Or do you have a vague feeling, perhaps even a memory, of having been abducted by aliens, or of travelling in a spaceship before being returned to wake in your own bed at home? Do you believe you can communicate telepathically with beings from other worlds while you sleep, waking up a little wiser or, alternatively, feeling a bit disconnected as if something is missing from your life? In summary, how do you feel about your alien encounters—are they real, or dreams?

They're dreams, symbolic dreams. They're about what feels alien or foreign to you. They're about experiences you have had that were so strange or difficult to understand that they might as well have happened on other planets. These dreams can also be about experiences where you were so hurt, emotionally or physically, that you despatched your pain far, far away, beyond your senses, beyond your everyday memory, beyond Planet You, only to return in dreams in vague, non-human form. Children with very strict religious upbringing often push natural beliefs and feelings—ones they have been taught to believe are evil—far, far away; disowning them.

These dreams use symbols that play on words. They introduce you to parts of your self or your life experiences that you have alienated, or they remind you that however far you banish certain experiences and feelings, however much you refuse to identify with them, they still hover, as UFOs—unidentified flying objects.

The experiences you have alienated may have been huge and awful, or they may have been small misunderstandings that you felt uncomfortable keeping on board. Welcome these dreams, and set about interpreting them using the other tips in this book, because they offer you the chance to have another look at what you have rejected. They help you to understand, heal, take back on board and then ground a part of yourself that has been hurt and missing, and nurse it back to health.

What did you banish from Planet You?

Tip 64
Earthquakes, shifting scenery and futuristic worlds

arthquake! The dream ground trembles beneath your feet, you feel shaky, unsure. What can you cling to for safety? What will shift, what will fall, what will remain the same? Maybe the tremors remain small, or maybe seas empty and mountains rise, or mountains sink and seas rise. Have you had this kind of dream?

You may have had similar dreams, not earthquakes, but shifting scenes. Roads or houses familiar to you, or once familiar to you, may shimmer and change before your eyes. New roads or buildings appear in their place, either entirely new, or combining parts of the old.

Or ordinary things become extraordinary. A plane transforms mid-flight into a futuristic flying machine, or you turn a page of a book to fall into a four dimensional world that defies description when you awake from your dream.

What these kinds of dreams have in common is shifting, morphing, and changing. These kinds of dreams come up when your understanding of the world and how it works is rapidly shifting. Your dreams reflect your experiences of seeing the world through new eyes.

The parts that are familiar represent your past way of seeing and understanding your world. The shaky, trembling, morphing parts represent your old beliefs and perceptions crumbling and changing. The futuristic parts reflect your experiences on the brink of what currently appears to be weird, wonderful, and way out. In the days and weeks to come, what seems weird to you now will become your new normal. It's at times like this that you look back on your life and realise that nothing stays the same, and that even your new, emerging perception of the world you live in will surely shift and change again and again in the future.

What do you feel in these dreams? Fear? Awe? What you feel in these dreams reflects how you are feeling about these changes in your life. The tip here is to be aware that your perceptions of the world are rapidly changing. Wait long enough for your new world to stop shaking and shimmering so you can get solid bearings before making any big decisions. These confusing yet exciting times will settle, and all will become clear.

Your understanding of the world is rapidly shifting

Tip 65
When the right side is different from the left

D o you see images, colours, or dreamlike visions when you have a massage? Have you noticed a difference between the types of images you see when the left side of your body is being massaged compared to the right? You'll most likely have observed that massaging the left side (or just your left foot) brings up more surreal and flowing images than the more literal and geometric ones brought up by massaging the right side (or right foot). Try it and see. (For some people, the left and right results are reversed.)

The reason for the difference between the two sides is that your right brain connects to the left side of your body, and your left brain connects to the right side. Your left brain pictures sensations in more literal or geometric images, while your right brain pictures sensations in more surreal, flowing forms. Massage triggers nerves and releases stored tensions in your body tissues. Your brain senses these and translates them into images.

Have you ever noticed a dramatic difference between left and right in some dreams? You might see an animal with one ear much bigger than the other, or see an industrial scene on your right and a magical world on your left, for example.

How should you interpret these differences or imbalances? To do this, you need to understand a little about your left and right brain.

Your right brain* is creative, intuitive, and emotional. It takes a holistic view of your world. It handles your inner world and your spiritual insights. It is more about being than doing. This also describes the energy of Yin, and is sometimes symbolised in dreams by women.

Your left brain* is rational, and literal, connected with your intellect. It takes a more mechanical view of your world, seeing it as a sum of its parts rather than something greater than the sum of its parts. It's more about doing than being. It handles your outer world. This also describes the energy of Yang, and is sometimes symbolised in dreams by men.

In dreams where there is an imbalance between left and right, interpret what is happening on the left in terms of right brain qualities. (Remember, the right brain connects to the left side of the body.) Apply left brain qualities to what is happening on the right side.

In short, look at the left side in dreams as your inner world, and the right side in dreams as your outer world. Interpret a big right ear in your dream, for example, as symbolising listening to your inner world, or a missing left leg as symbolising not having any standing, support, or direction in your outer world.

*Right and left are reversed for some people. This does not appear to be related to left and right-handedness.

Tip 66
Scenes from a movie, aka 'Blame it on the cheese'

oes the movie you watched last night, the cheese you ate after dinner, or the whisky you knocked back all evening affect your dreams? Might a hot night, a thunderstorm, a full bladder, a rattling window, a screeching mosquito, or a headache explain away a weird dream?

Yes, and then again, no! Let's start with the movie. If a movie really affects you, your dreaming mind will often process the parts that resonated with your emotions, personal issues, beliefs, and life experiences. Your dream may or may not use some of the symbols from the movie, but whatever the dream, do not dismiss it as caused by the movie. Think of the movie as having prompted issues that need your deeper attention.

How about that cheese or alcohol? The idea that cheese causes bad dreams is an old wives' tale, though body sensations such as indigestion, thirst, cold, a full bladder, a blocked nose, and numbness can get picked up by your brain and woven into the storyline of a dream. So your indigestion might turn up in a dream as a python coiling around your waist, the thirst as a shift in scene to a desert, the cold air as a passing ghost, or the numbness as a lost limb, but these will vary from person to person and from dream to dream. Again, the important thing is not to dismiss your dream as caused by the cheese, cold, or thirst, but to ask why your dream has chosen a certain symbol or way of processing the sensation. That symbol is meaningful, as is your dream. It tells you about how your mind works, and that's the object and power of dream interpretation.

The rattling window might become the sound of a roulette game in one person's dream, a cattle train speeding by in another person's dream, and a trash bin being emptied in someone else's dream. How the dreaming mind interprets the intrusion, and how it goes on to incorporate it into the dream storyline, delivers meaningful insight about the dreamer.

So never dismiss any dream. Oh, about the alcohol. Binge drinking can knock out dreams for a few hours, but if you sleep long enough you'll experience more intense dreams towards morning. It's as if the dreaming mind has to squeeze all the dreams in at the end of the night, once the worst of the alcohol is out of your system. These intense dreams are 'REM Rebound' dreams. REM is the normal dreaming phase. Too much alcohol blocks REM in the early hours so, come morning, it's rebound time. And, yes, those dreams are meaningful, so don't dismiss them.

Never dismiss a dream

Tip 67
Recipe for five-star dream sets

ou can increase the sensual quality and detail of your dreams by sharpening your sensual awareness while you are awake. But why do this?

There are two main reasons. The first is that a clear and detailed dream provides you with more information, when interpreted, than a hazy, vague one.

The second reason is purely hedonistic. If you're going to spend all those hours asleep and dreaming, why experience dreary two-star dream movies when you can go for full sense-around, insightful, five-star gold class?

Each night, your dreams process your conscious and unconscious experiences of the last 24–48 hours, so open yourself to full sensual awareness so that your dreaming mind has plenty of exciting material to work with.

Take a few minutes, for example, to stand under a tree and absorb the sights, sounds, and smells around you. Wait long enough for your busy mind to stop blocking the natural environment. Tune into the sounds of the birds and insects you hadn't noticed previously, and observe the way the wind ruffles the leaves in the trees. Pick a leaf and examine it closely, tracing the pattern of the veins, turning it over in your hand to watch subtle colour changes as the light dances over its surface. Close your eyes and feel the weight and texture of the leaf in your palm.

Extend the same sensual attention several times a day, perhaps eating slowly to extract every taste and texture of your food, or admiring the brushstrokes of a painting up close, or focussing on a particular word in an article you're reading long enough for the word to change shape, sound, and emphasis before your eyes. Speak the name of someone you love, over and over again, until it takes on new meaning.

The idea is to absorb and dissect as much sensual detail as you can while you are awake, beginning to sense your world in a whole new way. Your dreaming mind will follow through and deliver increased quality and detail in your dreams. Then it's over to you to enjoy ... and interpret.

Sense your world in a whole new way

Tip 68
Lucid dreams—when you are awake in a dream

There's a 'fact' you'll read in many dream books that states that you cannot switch on a light in a dream. You can, the theory goes, flick a light switch, but the light will not go on or off according to your desire in the dream. Dream experts often suggest that you use this light switch test to see if you are dreaming. Sounds bizarre? Here's the story.

How sure are you that you're not dreaming at this moment? Might you be dreaming that you're reading this dream tip? How can you test to see if you're dreaming? You could pinch yourself, but what would that prove? You can feel touch and pain in dreams too. Is there a better test?

But hang on a minute. When you're having a dream, do you ever question whether you're dreaming? You might dream about dreaming, or you might dream that you're talking to someone about dream interpretation, or you might even interpret a symbol in your dream, saying something like, "Oh, look! That clock's a great symbol for a timely face!" but do you ever question your reality and ask yourself if you could be dreaming?

When you suddenly become aware, in the middle of a dream, that you're dreaming, amazing possibilities open up. You can decide to do anything you wish, because you're safely tucked up in bed and dreaming. You can fly and fully experience the feeling, or summon up someone famous and spend time together that feels totally real— anything! This is 'Lucid Dreaming'. It's when you're aware that you are dreaming and yet the dream doesn't feel any less real than it did before you woke up to the fact. If anything, lucid dreaming feels more real, because you can really turn up your senses. However, there's one vital trap here. What if you're wrong? What if you decide you're dreaming, and jump off a tall building to fly—but you're actually awake? This is why you need a perfect test.

The light switch test is not good. Many people can turn lights on and off effectively in dreams. A better idea is to invent your own dream symbol, something that could not possibly exist in waking life. Imagine looking at your right hand and seeing six fingers, for example. This would confirm you were dreaming. To make this work, look at your right hand many times a day, imagining a sixth finger. If you really focus on this, your dreaming mind will eventually bring it into your dream because it's something new to explore. You may dream of looking at your hand, see the sixth finger, and not remember this is the sign you're looking for, but one day the magic will happen and you will take the cue and realise you are lucid dreaming.

You might still want to exercise caution, perhaps launching into flight from the ground rather than from a high building, but enjoy! Waking life will never be the same again.

8

Predicting the future in dreams

Tip 69
Blueprint of the future

ell your dream to a friend. Okay, so not everyone is interested in dreams, but some are, and if you find someone to swap dreams with, this exercise will work really well for both of you.

Tell your dream to a friend, and then ask him to summarise your dream in no more than a couple of sentences. Listen carefully to those two sentences. Perhaps even write them down. For example, the summary might be something like, "You are lost and can't find your way. You keep going round in circles", or "You want to fly higher but people keep saying you can't."

Ask your friend how he sees that summary applying to your life. Then ask yourself how that summary applies to your life. Between the two of you, you'll strike gold.

A friend, just one step removed from your situation, can often see more clearly than you.

Once you see the pattern of your life—the blueprint of your future—you can change it, if you wish. Become the pattern maker, not the pattern.

Become the pattern maker, not the pattern

Tip 70
Can dreams predict death?

What should you do if you dream of the death of someone close to you, perhaps even you? This dream is so frightening that people often believe it is a glimpse of the future, especially if the dream mentions an age or date.

Can such dreams be precognitive? Well, if you wait long enough, yes, since we all die in the end, though dreams giving ages or dates will mostly be wildly inaccurate! There are some extremely rare incidences of people accurately dreaming of their own death, or the deaths of others, but rest assured that this dream is common and also symbolic. Ask around. Most people regularly dream of illness, death, or dying, and many people have specifically dreamed of their own death or the death of someone close, with everyone concerned alive and well for years to come to tell the tale.

Instead of preparing for a funeral, look within, as death in a dream is symbolic of what is ending in your life. Ask what is ending for you: a period of study, a relationship, an attitude, an old belief or way of looking at the world, a phase of life, or your cash flow, for example?

Endings can be good; without endings, new beginnings are difficult. So wherever you are ready for change in your life, you may first find you need to let something end. This is why dreams of death are common during periods of change. It's sad when the old dies, but necessary. In dreams about timely endings, you feel sad but okay about the death.

But endings are not always appropriate. You might be giving up that study or relationship too early, for example. Maybe you should be breathing more life into it, instead of watching it die. Be guided by your feelings and other clues in your death dreams, to understand the changes you are going through, and to make decisions about the future.

Also see Tip 71

Death dreams are normal in times of change

Tip 71
Can dreams predict dates?

hen a dream gives you a date or an age, perhaps for a death, a wedding, a birth, a conception, or a job offer, can you take the dream as an accurate prediction of your future? Should you draw up a will, book time off work for your honeymoon, decide on baby names, or plan your new professional wardrobe?

On extremely rare occasions, a dream may give accurate details of a future event, including dates, but if you have a date dream, don't make any plans. Jot down the dream to compare with future events if you like, but it is far more practical and insightful to interpret these dreams symbolically. If weddings, births, and new jobs are on your wish list, the best way to bring them into your life is to understand yourself through your dreams so that you can make the changes within you that attract the people and events you desire.

Your dreaming mind accurately accesses dates from your memory, including dates from your past and other more general dates that you have remembered from history or current affairs. It will use these dates as symbols. For example, if a childhood pet died on September 16 one year, this date might come up in a dream dealing with grief or loss of something precious. If you once got a fabulous new job on May 10, then whenever you are dreaming about rewards—or lack of them—your dream might use this date to symbolise 'good news', or rewards, or any feelings you associated when you first got that new job.

Far from predicting the future, these date dreams link something that is happening in your life today to a feeling or issue from your past, the date being a clue. Ponder the clue and look for connections, though understand that your dream may have dredged up a date long since lost to your conscious mind.

If you dream you will die on November 30, for example, you may look back and remember a November 30 ten years ago when something ended (died) in your life, such as a relationship, expectation, or period of study. Instead of predicting your death, ask what is ending in your life today that feels similar to what happened back then.

If you dream you will die at age 62, look at this symbolically too. Did someone you know die at 62? What happened to you in 1962, or when you lived at a number 62, or when you used to catch a number 62 bus, or when you once got 62% in an exam? Unfortunately, your dreams don't always make interpretation easy. Your unconscious mind is complex and clever, but when you do find the right connection, you feel it as a deep, goose-bumpy 'Aha' recognition. At that point, your dream suddenly makes sense, and you feel enormous relief because you then know, absolutely, that death is not banging at your door.

Tip 72
That reminds me of my dream …

ave you heard the old expression, 'That broke my dream'? Breaking a dream was considered a sign of good luck. It meant something came up during the day that reminded you of your dream the night before. So, if you'd dreamed of a cow wearing a pink bell around its neck, and the next day you were flicking through a magazine and noticed a picture of a pink bell, you'd say, "That broke my dream!" Or if you'd dreamed of an old friend, and that friend phoned you the next day, you might say, "You broke my dream!"

Today we might call these synchronicities, serendipities, or precognitive dreams, depending on how amazed we feel by the event. In the old-fashioned sense, though, even an everyday event like putting on the kettle—the same old kettle you put on every morning—could break your dream if it suddenly reminded you of a dream you had completely forgotten until that moment. "Oh," you might say, "I've just remembered a dream I had last night! A genie appeared from the spout of my kettle!" Given that it's unlikely that a genie will actually appear from your kettle in waking life, this is not a synchronicity or a precognitive dream. (Though imagine how much good luck you'd have if a real genie broke your dream and granted you three wishes!) So, what does it mean if this happens to you, and what good luck can it bring?

When someone or something breaks a dream that you had already remembered and recorded in your journal, go back and look at your interpretation again, really focussing on that symbol. The event gives it extra significance.

When a dream you had not recalled suddenly flashes into your memory, take careful note of the 'break'-through event that tripped your recall. Ask what you were feeling, or what issue was unfolding for you at that moment. Your dream was probably dealing with that feeling or issue. The waking life feeling or issue resonated with the same feeling or issue in your dream, and brought back the memory. What good luck! You can return to interpret your dream, confidently knowing the subject matter. If the 'break'-through event was contentious, you also know your dream holds the key— the breakthrough—to handling that kind of situation in the future. Who needs a genie, especially when you are fast becoming your very own dream-genie through using these dream tips?

Also see Tips 73, 74, 75, 76

When synchronicity calls, listen

Tip 73
When dreams come true—literally

an your dreams foretell the shape of things to come? And, if they can, is there anything you can do to change that future?

On extremely rare occasions, events in waking life unfold exactly as previewed in a dream. When this happens, detail matches detail with stunning accuracy, and there is no room for doubt. These are cases of literal precognition (literal prediction), where the event matches the dream literally. While most people never have this experience, others find this occurs several times a year throughout their lives, or in occasional runs.

The only way to prove a literal precognitive dream is to record all your dreams on waking and then compare these to the actual events. Most literal precognitive dreamers find their highest accuracy applies to events in their personal lives (rather than to world events), and these are most likely to occur in the first ten days, but especially in the first 24–48 hours.

What should you do if you believe you have just had a literal precognitive dream, and, supposing it is, can you change the outcome?

Even precognitive dreamers have huge difficulty knowing which of their dreams will happen. Given that we all dream around five dreams a night, and a literal precognitive dreamer experiences maybe up to five accurate literal precognitive dreams a year, you can see that most dreams are not literal predictions. As many of the tips in this book point out, common dreams of death, accidents, and other horrific scenarios involving ourselves, our families, and loved ones plague us all—and are entirely symbolic.

Interpret your dream as a normal symbolic dream. When it begins to make perfect sense, you will start to feel relief. If you attend to what the dream is revealing about your inner world, you discover deeply meaningful information that empowers you to change your personal future. Remember, too, that the surest way to change the world is to begin by changing yourself. As you change, you see the world differently. As you change, other people experience a different 'you', and they respond and change accordingly, touched by you as surely as ripples from a pebble thrown into a pond touch distant shores.

If a rare dream does turn out to come true, and the outcome upsets you, remember that your dream preview was a privilege, perhaps helping you to accept that some outcomes may be destined. It's important to realise that if you put all your energy into trying to stop dreams from manifesting, you risk great psychiatric distress. Remember the statistics. Only the tiniest fraction of dreams will come true literally. Put your energies into evolving personally and spiritually by interpreting your dreams symbolically, and acting upon your insights to make yourself—and the world—a better place.

Far more interesting than literal precognitive dreams is the fact that most dreams are symbolically precognitive, as the next tip reveals.

Also see Tips 72, 74, 75, 76

Tip 74
When dreams come true—symbolically

o dreams catch glimpses of the shape of things to come? Tip 73 discussed the very rare phenomenon of dreams that come true exactly as previewed in the dream. These types of dreams are known as literal precognitive (literal predictive) dreams.

More common are symbolic precognitive (symbolic predictive) dreams. For example, you might have a dream about death, and in the days following the dream, you notice things in your life ending (death), such as the end of a project, relationship, or money supply. That ending may be good (the project is finally finished!) or not so good (you thought the relationship would last forever). Or you might dream that a tree is bearing ripe fruit. In the days following the dream, you might receive surprise news of a windfall from an investment you'd forgotten about, or you might discover you are pregnant.

It's as if your unconscious mind detects the way the wind is blowing in your life, and pictures this symbolically in a dream. The big question is, is the wind blowing in a certain direction in your life because of destiny, or because you are manifesting it? Was your relationship destined to end, or did you create its ending? Is your future set, or is it your call, with the way things are shaping up previewed symbolically in your dreams?

Whether or not some parts of your future are preordained, experience suggests over and over again that we are the masters of our own destiny. Dreams are exceptional tools in helping you to see what destiny you are creating. Symbolic precognitive dreams are especially helpful in bringing this to your attention.

In other words, if you understand your dream symbols, you can predict the shape of things to come in your life and, if you wish, change that future. The magic is to catch a glimpse of a pattern as it is forming in your dreams—to notice the blueprint you are creating —and then choose to let it manifest, or help it to manifest faster, or change its course. You can do all of this by working with your dream symbols once you understand their meaning and there are plenty of tips in this book showing you how to do this.

When you wake from a dream, ask, "Which way is the wind blowing in my dream, and what pattern is it creating?" You might conclude, "The wind is blowing in the direction of things ripening, creating a pattern of readiness to harvest." Then be your own psychic and predict the harvest you are creating, as previewed in your dream. Oh, and after making your prediction, decide whether you want to accept that future harvest, or plough it back into the earth in favour of a different outcome. The choice is yours.

Also see Tips 72, 73, 75, 76

Tip 75
When your dream symbols appear in waking life

hat does it mean when symbols from a dream start appearing in waking life? Here's what usually happens.

You have a dream featuring, for example, a red bucket. You wake in the morning and trip over your toddler's toy red bucket in the hall. You dismiss this, thinking you must have seen the bucket there before you went to bed. Later that morning, you find a flyer tucked under your windscreen wiper. It features a red bucket, and turns out to be an ad for a hardware store. You smile and think, "That's odd!" Stopped at the lights, a boy asks if you'd like your windscreen washed. He carries a red bucket of water. And when you go to the movies that evening, you are presented with a complimentary giant serve of popcorn in a red bucket-shaped container. By now, the appearance of so many red buckets in one day seems eerily significant and deeply meaningful, only you have absolutely no idea what they mean. This phenomenon is synchronicity.

The interesting thing is that some dreams produce far more synchronicities than you might normally notice. The theme of a dream is its 'motif'. If you look deeper, you'll often see your motif dream symbol repeating the next day in modified or cryptic forms. Here's an example.

Imagine you dreamed of a 'memory stick' computer accessory. The next day, you hear someone on the radio talking about memory sticks, then you see an article on memory titled 'When memory sticks'. An hour later, you notice a child playing a memory-improving game featuring stick-like figures. At work you keep getting someone's name wrong (as if your memory is stuck), and at home in the evening a CD sticks, repeating the same piece of music. Only one of these synchronicities looks anything like a memory stick, but the others are equally significant echoes of the dream motif.

Sometimes you experience the synchronicities in the absence of a dream, or so you think. In these cases, it is most likely that you have simply not recalled the dream. So what does synchronicity mean?

When you experience synchronicity, go back to the dream and interpret it thoroughly, because the dream theme is so powerful that it is already symbolically manifesting in your life. Yes, this is another example of symbolic precognition (see Tip 74).

Many people think of synchronicity as a positive sign to follow. They will follow red buckets and memory sticks as if they lead to pots of gold. But synchronicity is not necessarily a sign to follow. It is a symbol shouting loudly from your dream, spilling into your waking life. It is the symbolic beginning of a manifestation. If you interpret your dream and you like the way the wind is blowing, follow the signs. If you don't like the way the wind is blowing, check tip 74 and change your future.

Also see Tips 74, 76

Tip 76
Telepathy in dreams

an you tune into people or events in your dreams? Can you read people's minds, or visit or interact with them while you are dreaming?

Tips 73 and 74 have already explored predictive dreams where you glimpse the future. The question here is not about glimpsing or predicting the future, but about discovering what is happening in the same time scale, while you are dreaming. It's about telepathic dreaming, about accessing someone else's mind telepathically. It is about extrasensory perception in the present. Well, having defined it, is it a real phenomenon?

Have you ever dreamed of an event and then read about it in the newspaper the next day? When you think back, you'll often discover that the event happened before or during your dream. You might have woken up in the morning and said, "I dreamed the president was murdered." On reading 'President murdered' as the headline in the morning's paper, you might have thought, "I had a precognitive dream!" In a way, you did, because you foresaw yourself, in the future, reading this news, but it is more likely that you tuned into the mind of someone (or many people) involved in writing up the story and producing the news, if not the actual event itself.

In many cases where people believe they have had a precognitive dream and recorded it, closer examination reveals that the event happened while they were asleep, or at least one other person knew about it even though the dreamer did not. Examples include dreaming of a birth, death, or the contents of an email or letter already in the mail but not yet received. Other examples are inventions, laws, or movie scripts in the making, yet to be revealed to the public. These kinds of dreams, containing information that the dreamer could not possibly have known, have proven accurate so many times. Telepathic dreaming happens. It is more common than precognitive dreaming. In fact, when many precognitive dreams are explored, they turn out to have been telepathic.

If people can dream telepathically in this way, then they can dream telepathically about people they know, about what they are thinking, doing, or planning.

The danger is in believing that all your dreams featuring people you know are telepathic. The rule of thumb is that most dreams are about you, and the people who feature in your dreams represent your beliefs about them. What you believe about a person says more about you than about them, so you stand to gain most insight into yourself—and your relationship with the other—by interpreting your dream symbolically.

Nevertheless, why do we sometimes tune into other people telepathically through our dreams? Sometimes it's because there's a strong emotional connection. Sometimes it's because there's a symbolic connection, for example you may tune into a mountaineer conquering a mountain when you are conquering a huge challenge in your own life. Either way, telepathic dreaming is still about you, so interpret all your dreams!

Also see Tip 43

Tip 77
Sharing the same dream

What does it mean if your dreams overlap with your partner's, or with a friend's? Are you dreaming the other person's dream, are they dreaming yours, are you dream sharing, or is it simply coincidental?

If you share your life closely with another person, you may often dream similar themes because you discuss or experience similar situations. If you and your partner share a crisis on the same day, it's likely that you'll both dream about it, and your dreams may use similar symbols or reflect the same emotional themes.

If you share a creative problem with a friend, you may both take it into your dreams to explore, searching for a solution. So you may both dream similar symbols or themes, though you may each come up with different solutions.

As discussed in Tip 76, some people tune in during their dreams to what is happening for other people. Sometimes this happens while both people are dreaming, so that one ends up tuning into parts of the other person's dreams, incorporating symbols or themes into their own unique dream. If the two of you suspect this, you'll enjoy endless discussions about who is tuning into whom, comparing times of dreams.

Here's an experiment or a bit of fun you can try if you want to experience shared dreaming. This works on the principle that your dreams tend to address anything unusual that you focus on during the day and just prior to sleep.

Pick a specific symbol, for example a blue star. Discuss the blue star with your partner for this experiment during the day. Keep returning to the subject, together and alone. Become obsessive about it for a day. Picture it as you fall asleep.

Compare notes with your dream partner. If you both dreamed of the blue star, look for other similarities in your dreams. If you are not linked telepathically during dreams, the dreams will probably be quite different apart from the blue star. If you are linked telepathically during dreams, there may be a higher similarity between the dreams, though this is not really conclusive as you may just be similarly wired.

It's a fun exercise, but what it really shows is that even if you are sharing dream symbols with other people, your individual dreaming minds usually mould the symbols into individual dream scenarios. Bob might dream of his fear of failing to see the blue star in his dream, and Nick might dream of the day his teacher gave him a blue star instead of a gold star when he was five. The moral of this story, and the tip? The bottom line is that even if you are dreaming telepathically, your dream will simply incorporate that symbol you picked up from the other person's dream into your own personal drama. So, for maximum personal insight, interpret all your dreams!

Also see Tip 76

9

Dreaming of the past

Tip 78
Why does the past haunt your dreams?

o you dream of a childhood home, of your school, a job you once had, or an ex who was once not quite so ex? Why does the past haunt your dreams, and how can you use these kinds of dreams to focus more on today and your future?

It's as simple as this. The past can hold you back. To move forward in life you often need to release yourself from the past.

As a child, you learn your basic beliefs about the world from your parents, your school, and your early experiences. You acquire certain attitudes and fears about the world, and, although these change through your teenage years, they tend to get pretty set in concrete by adulthood. What you do in life depends on your fears, your attitudes, and your beliefs about yourself and about life.

When your dreams show you symbols from your past, they are showing you where your past is influencing your present. Let your mind wander over those past symbols until you see a connection between how you felt about life back then and how you feel about life now. You'll be amazed at what you learn about yourself.

*Your dreams reveal where your past
is influencing your present*

Tip 79
The gift of hindsight

The past can look so different in hindsight. Difficulties you experienced as a young teenager may make you smile now. Why exactly was it that talking to someone of the opposite sex was so hard? And why did you tremble in front of a particular teacher when you can clearly see, looking back, that she was scared of her students? And what about that relationship break-up? In hindsight, you can see it wouldn't have lasted, and you feel much more compassion for what your ex went through at the time.

Hindsight is a blessing, granted bit by bit, year by year, insight by insight. Your dreams can help you to view your past through different eyes, to reconstruct the story of your life according to your growing wisdom and understanding, to make better sense of it all. Your progress is often pictured in dreams by changes made to houses you once lived in. These very common dreams are symbolic reconstructions of your past.

In a dream revisiting a childhood home, for example, you might notice that the whole house has been widened and opened up to let in more light. On waking and thinking about how real your dream seems, you may be tempted to drive past the old home and see if you've tuned into recent renovations, but these dreams are symbolic. Your dream shows the changes that have occurred within you since those childhood days. You have opened up the past to let more light in.

Or perhaps that childhood home, in a dream, has had walls knocked down symbolising the barriers you've overcome since then, or maybe it's surrounded by a high fence symbolising your hindsight understanding that your family were defensive and overly protective, an insight that helps put your life today into context.

Let your dreams show you the difference between how the past felt for you at the time, and how you see it now. Let hindsight help you to free yourself to see your way forward.

Reconstruct the story of your life

Tip 80
Hugs, warm embraces and sex

I f you've ever spent a dreaming night hugging or receiving hugs from people from your past, you'll know how refreshed, loved, and supported you feel on waking in the morning. Just one loving dream embrace can be enough to get you off to a good start the next day.

But what if that friendly loving hugging turns into cuddling and escalates into sex? The chances are that you'll still wake up feeling refreshed, loved, and supported until your brain kicks in and you reel back in disbelief. How could you have enjoyed sex with someone beyond the boundaries of your sexual preference or, worse still, with a close relation, an act regarded as incest in waking life? Does this kind of dream reveal hidden sexual desires or deviances?

The short answer is no. This kind of dream is very common, and despite the extreme discomfort you may feel when you wake up and think about it, in most cases the dream experience itself is positive and healing. The key to understanding this is to take a big breath, relax, and remember that people and events in your dreams are symbolic. So what do these dreams mean?

Forget sex for a moment, and focus on those lovely, innocent, friendly, hugging dreams. Each hug generally represents a healing for you. For example, if you felt hurt by Jack in the past, or if you felt you hurt Jack, then hugging Jack in a dream usually occurs when you have forgiven him, or forgiven yourself, for that long ago hurt. If you had unresolved business with someone and you find yourself embracing him in a dream, it's usually because you have reached a sense of peace. You can't go back to the past, you may not be able to contact a person today, and it may not be appropriate to contact someone who may not be ready for such an encounter, but you can resolve and heal an issue or disquiet within yourself. A dream hug with the person who represents that unfinished business signals your healing is complete.

Where you had no particular issues with someone from your past and he still turns up in your dream to embrace you, ask what strengths or weaknesses you saw in him, as your dream suggests you are embracing, acknowledging, and healing these qualities within yourself now.

So let's now add the sex back in. Sex is an extreme embrace. In these dreams, as long as the sex felt good and your emotions felt positive in the dream, distance yourself from the waking life implications and just know that your dream sex was an extreme healing. Oh, and if your dream sex partner was someone unknown to you from your past, just ask what strengths or weaknesses that person seemed to have in the dream, because these are the qualities you are embracing, acknowledging, and healing within yourself in your dream.

Also see Tip 43

Tip 81
Can you dream of past lives?

f your dream is set in a time before you were born, does it give you insight into a past life? Sometimes people dream of being themselves as they appear today, only in historic dress to suit the period, and sometimes people dream they look quite different, or are of the opposite sex, clearly at one with the time period and not realising it is a past era until they wake up. How should you interpret these kinds of dreams?

When these dreams lack surreal oddities, when they feel everyday except that everyday was long ago, it's very tempting to conclude that you experienced a past-life memory in a dream. Who's to say? You may have, you may not have. But before you go too far down this track, beware! Think of all the dreams you've had featuring your childhood, perhaps your childhood home, school, family life, or holiday camp. These dreams contain a mix of accurate detail and oddities, don't they? Your childhood home might look more or less the same but have an extra room, back onto a beach instead of a suburban garden, or have a fairy living in the cupboard. Dreams are not what they seem.

There have been many distressing cases where people have dreamed of being sexually abused in settings similar to their childhood home or school, and, because the dreams seemed so real, concluded they had indeed been abused, moving on to make accusations against innocent people. While memories can and do surface in dreams, it's vital to understand that most dream content is entirely symbolic. The same applies to dreams set in historic periods before your birth.

Interpret the historic era in your dream as symbolic. If you dream you're a soldier in a war, ask what personal conflict you're fighting today. If you dream you're being persecuted as a witch in the Middle Ages, ask what you're feeling persecuted about today, or how you feel about being middle aged. Or simply summarise the historic dream setting or era in one word such as 'stuffy', 'liberated', 'pioneering', 'enslaved', or 'pagan', and ask which area of your life this applies to today.

Dreams are not what they seem

Tip 82
Back at school

Just how many times do you need to sit that test? This common dream finds you back at your old school, or a dream school, about to sit a test. Usually, something goes wrong. You're unprepared, you are given the wrong paper, you can't read the questions, your pen won't write, or you run out of time. If you're lucky, you might just remember towards the end of the dream that you're no longer of school age, and you may even remember that you've passed this exam and even exams at a much higher level. Thankful and relieved, you realise you no longer need to be at this school, so you leave. Less fortunate dreamers only find relief upon awakening.

When you have this dream, ask where in your life today you have been feeling tested, or anxious about performing or living up to someone else's expectations. Are you responding to this situation in the same way you did when you were back at school?

Think back to your school days and the kinds of things that were important to you back then, and ask if those things are still affecting you today.

Deep down inside, are you still trying to impress that old teacher, the one who upset you so long ago? Or, as a school child, did you try to win your parents' approval by doing well in exams, and are you still, in your life today, feeling a need to win the approval of other authority figures?

A variation of this dream is the one where you have to give a presentation in your adult world. Again, things go wrong. Your laptop isn't working, the microphones are dead, you've forgotten what you wanted to say, your clothes are all wrong, no one's turned up to hear you, or your audience is booing you or walking out. Ask where other people's judgement of you has become important, and why you have let this happen. Or are you judging yourself too harshly? It may be time to set yourself new standards, standards that bring more love, joy, and balance into your life.

What brings out the schoolchild in you?

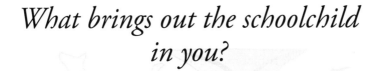

Tip 83
When yesterday's work spills into your dreams

ork, work, work. You work all day at a task and then, just when you could do with a break, what do you dream? More of the same—work, work, work. How can you get a well-deserved break while you sleep? How can you get some of the exciting dreams other people enjoy?

There are two main types of boring work dreams.

In the first type, you dream you do the same repetitive task you do all day long at work. In these dreams there's very little difference between work and dream. Nothing exciting happens beyond the odd obstacle that sometimes makes your work more difficult than it is in reality.

This dream usually comes up for jobs where the task never seems to be done. You clean something, it gets dirty. You satisfy one customer only for the next one to appear. You complete one cycle of work only to be back at the beginning of another one, much the same. Nothing seems to evolve or change. When this seems to be the case at work, your dreaming mind often goes over and over the scenario trying to solve what feels stuck. Life is about evolving, learning, moving forward, and your dreams work to solve situations in your life where this is not happening. When you have this dream, ask how you can introduce change into your life, how you can stimulate personal evolution. The solution might be as simple as learning to see your job, or your life, in a new way. Once things start to change for you, more exciting or restful dreams will take their place.

The second type of boring work dream is where a new task or project you've just started reappears in your dream for more attention, just when you needed a brain rest.

This type of dream is actually doing you a big favour. Your dreaming brain looks for creative solutions to the problems you are working on, or simply practises your new skills, doing a bit of overtime training. Your dream solutions may be brilliant in the dream and useless when you wake up, but don't forget that they are symbolic. Your waking brain soon finds the unscrambled version, created and filed away by your dream during the night. Have you noticed how many times you've slept on a problem only to wake with the perfect, creative remedy? You have your dreams to thank for that.

If you really don't want to dream of work, write a list early in the evening of any unfinished work tasks, and a 'to do' action list to cover each of them. Then spend the evening encouraging non-work thoughts and relaxing. Your dreams usually start by addressing what is on your mind as you fall asleep, so make those last waking moments work for you.

Tip 84
Guilty—if only in your dreams

he sirens are flashing and the police are on their way. That body you buried so long ago is coming to the surface. You got away with it for all those years, but your past is catching up with you now, and you're guilty. Or maybe the authorities haven't been alerted just yet, but some misgiving is surfacing in your dream and you are so glad to wake up and discover that you didn't do it. You're innocent, after all. What a relief.

But are you? What is innocence, and what is guilt? Who's to judge what's right or wrong? Okay, so most people might agree that killing someone and burying the body might be on the wrong side, but remember, dreams are symbolic and dramatic. That dead body you buried in your dream may symbolise anything you buried, or hid from sight, in the past. For example, you might have buried your skills as a healer, and you might be feeling remorseful about that now. Or you might have buried your memories of a love affair, and these may be surfacing now, stirred up by recent events, bringing up feelings of guilt about the affair, or guilt for ending it. Or your guilt may extend right back to early childhood when you were made to feel irresponsible for an action, or inappropriately blamed for someone's circumstance.

When your dreams play dramas about being found out, or feelings of guilt, ask where in your life today you fear being exposed in some way, or you feel guilty about something.

If you draw a blank, your dream is most likely bringing up your feelings of guilt or remorse from the past, especially if your dream images suggest emergence from long ago, such as a long dead body working its way to the surface, or old buildings, old style cars or fashions, or people from your past.

Feelings of guilt, even when you deny them and bury them deep in your unconscious mind, can and do affect the way you live your life today. Guilt holds you back from moving forward. Guilt can cause you to punish yourself, even unconsciously, today and in the future. If you want to move forward in every area of your life, it's time to cut free from the strings of guilt. How can you do this?

First, recognise that there is no such thing as right or wrong. Judgement is in the eye of the beholder. Everyone does what feels right or justified at the time. It's only when you look back that you may judge differently. Second, apply forgiveness. This may mean forgiving yourself, or it may mean forgiving other people for blaming you and making you feel guilty for your innocent actions. Close your eyes and forgive yourself or others at the age you or they were back then. Feel it. Add love. Let go.

Cut free from the strings of guilt

Tip 85
In the land of giants

D o you have dreams where you seem to be living with giants in a giant's house? Do door handles seem too high, and beds too difficult to climb into? Does the family dog look like it's eaten massive doses of growth hormone? When you sit up to the table to eat, does your food appear on a plate the size of a serving platter and hover around shoulder height? Do you have to lift your spoon to eat? Spoon? Where's your knife and fork? Do the giants persist in talking way above your head, hardly noticing you down there, looking up to them?

Have you worked out what this kind of dream might mean? Here are a few more clues. Have you experienced, in a dream, suddenly being pulled up into the air and seeing things from a different perspective? Have you gone for a walk and had to reach up high to hold hands with one of the friendly giants who steered your course? Have you found yourself up close to the face of a giant and wondered at its sheer size? Or have you found yourself crawling on all fours when everyone else seems to be getting around normally?

You may have experienced one or more of these when your dreaming mind flashed back to the way you saw and experienced the world when you were a small child. Beware interpreting these dreams literally though. Dreams are symbolic, so whatever happened in your dream is not a replay of an actual memory, but a symbolic dream revealing that sometimes you still feel like a child in an adult's world, or that the way you see the world today is sometimes coloured by your childhood experiences.

When you have this kind of dream, ask where in your life today you feel more like a child than an adult, and what beliefs and attitudes you would need to change within yourself to interact on an adult-to-adult basis. If you draw a blank at answering these questions, look for clues in your dream to help you see which of the beliefs you picked up as a child are still influencing the way you live your life today. Are you happy with these, or is it time to give the child within a new set of beliefs more suited to living in an adult world?

When do you feel small?

Tip 86
A child in adult's clothing

Many dreams reveal beliefs you learned in the past that affect the way you live your life today. In an ideal world, we would all adjust our beliefs as we grow and experience the world in different ways. For example, as a child you might have acquired the belief from your parents that rich people are selfish. In your teenage years, you might have learned at school of many rich people who anonymously and unselfishly do good deeds for people in need. You may have met the rich parents of a school friend and noticed how unselfish they were. Ideally, you would adjust your belief about rich people accordingly. Your dreams help you to do this by comparing your new experiences with your old beliefs, replacing the original beliefs where the evidence seems overwhelming.

The problem is that our earliest beliefs have such a strong hold that they are sometimes very difficult to replace. It's as if your dreaming mind holds up the evidence, 'Look, those rich people you met today were so unselfish,' and then counters this with, 'Ah but, it says here, in your belief files, that rich people are selfish, so this must be true'.

One factor that is good at toppling old beliefs is emotional intensity. If you experience a trauma or strong emotional experience, it can be intense enough to replace an old belief with a new one. For example, if your partner of thirty years suddenly leaves you for someone much younger, the emotional shock may rapidly change your old belief that you are worthy of being loved into a new belief that you are unworthy of being loved.

At times when things are not working well for you the old inappropriate beliefs may be the culprits, especially when those beliefs are unconscious. Following the examples given in this tip, an unconscious belief that rich people are selfish might be stopping you from becoming rich, or a belief that you are not worthy of being loved might stop you from attracting a new partner.

Examine your dreams for signs of beliefs that are holding you back. There are plenty of tips in this book showing you how to do this. When you've identified a belief from your past that you'd like to change, close your eyes and visualise giving back the belief to the person who originally gave it to you. For example, you might give back to your mother the belief that rich people are selfish. Lovingly tell her, in your visualisation, that she is entitled to her belief, but you don't want it for yourself anymore. Hug her, feel the love, tell her your new belief, and add a strong emotion of joyful release to anchor it home.

Break the mould

Tip 87
Beware the victim

eware this trap. It's the trap of making excuses for the way your life is today, based on what your dreams reveal. This is how easily it can happen.

When you interpret your dreams you'll discover many beliefs you carry from your past, beliefs that help explain how your life has been up to this point. For example, through interpreting your dreams you might discover that you have a belief that it's selfish to speak up for what you want, following some negative experiences you had as a child when you tried to express your needs and wishes. You might think, "Aha! That explains a lot about my life today! It explains why I'm so shy." The trap is then saying, "I am shy because this or that happened in my childhood", or "It's because of what happened in my childhood that I'm too shy to ask for what I want in my life today." There's the trap. You're settling for shyness and suffering from 'Victim Mentality'. If you think like this, you'll always be a victim, a prisoner of your past.

The point of dream interpretation is not to wallow in your past, but to visit it to find keys to unlock doors to a better future. Instead of saying, "It's because of what happened in my childhood that I'm too shy to ask for what I want in my life today," say, "It's because of what happened in my childhood that I have been too shy to ask for what I want in my life until now. Now I see things clearly! That belief is not doing me any good. It's time to change that belief. I'm ready to believe that it's good to speak up for what I want and it's good to express myself and be heard."

There are plenty of tips throughout this book to show you how to change negative beliefs into positive ones. These include Tip 86 on how to give back a belief, and many other tips on using dream alchemy visualisations that communicate directly with your unconscious mind to change negative beliefs that work against you into positive beliefs that work for you.

No excuses, no blame, no victim mentality. Let dream interpretation empower you to understand the path that led you to this place, to be thankful for the experiences and life lessons you learned along the way, and to choose your future from this point forward.

Also see Tip 86

Dream interpretation frees you from the past

Tip 88
Checklist

All the tips in this section, and many throughout this book, reveal how your dreams go back to your past to highlight events, feelings, and beliefs that are powerfully affecting your life today. In many cases, these experiences from your past are holding you back from success.

It would be wonderful if dreams were straightforward, listing literal historic details of your past, but they're symbolic, and so the detective work is up to you. Here's a checklist to help you hunt for clues to pinpoint those past experiences so you can make sense of your life today.

Numbers: Remove any zeroes; they're just the dream's way of grabbing your attention. So make $7,200 into '72'. The clue might be 1972; when you lived at number 72; or when you used to take a number 72 bus. Or 5 might be a clue to when you were 5: five years ago; five months or weeks ago; or when you were in grade 5. Play with numbers till you hit gold.

Ages: Guess the ages of the key characters. These could be clues to when you were that age, or to that number of years ago.

Fashions and styles: Check clothes, buildings, music, technology, transport, food, and other dream details for clues.

People: When did you last see this person? When did you first meet this person? What do you have in common with this person? (For example, he is a real estate agent and you used to work in a real estate agency in what year?)

Pets: When did this pet come into your life? When did it die? Did it always accompany you at a certain time?

Cars: When did you have this car? When did you replace this car? Who did you know who had a car like this, and when? When was this car popular?

Houses: When did you live in this house? When was this style popular?

Your children or parents: How old are they in the dream? When were they that age? When were you that age?

The detective work is up to you

10

Guidance from dreams

Tip 89
The mirror and the compass

Are you looking for guidance from your dreams? Clear direction? A message to follow? People often think of dreams as being messages from a higher source, delivering an action plan for success.

It's true that you can find guidance and life-direction by interpreting a dream. You can even come up with a brilliant action plan for success, follow it, and achieve that success. But ... you knew there was a 'but' coming, didn't you? Here it is.

It is more accurate to say that your dreams tell you everything you need to know about who you are TODAY, how you see the world today, and why this is so. Your dreams often look back and remind you of your past experiences and relate them to what is happening for you today, because your past has shaped who you are today and how you see the world today. Your past—and today—also shapes who you will be tomorrow, and how you will see the world tomorrow, IF YOU LET IT!

Think of a dream as being a snapshot of you taken today. Of course, you need to be able to interpret your dream first to understand that snapshot, to see the big picture of you and your life as it is today. When you know how to do this, you really begin to understand yourself deeply and clearly, and this puts you in a position of great power.

Your dreams, once interpreted, give you a deeper view of yourself than you can get from any other method of self-understanding. Dreams show you your unconscious beliefs, feelings, attitudes, and ways of seeing the world. These will surprise you, at first, and then you will clearly see how they relate to your life. They explain why your life is the way it is today.

When you understand yourself as you are today, you have the power to change, to create a new you and a new way of seeing the world for tomorrow. Instead of repeating the same old cycles, going round in circles through the same old experiences, you can break free and move forward to the life you really want. That's the power and the magic of dream interpretation.

So don't look for direct guidance from your dreams. Instead, look into the mirror of your dreams to understand your position TODAY so clearly that you can make changes and set your compass to move towards the future you choose.

Choose your future and set your compass

Tip 90
A guide to magic

Some dreams are uplifting and inspiring, and some, well, they just need a little magic to turn them—and something in your life—around. You can do that magic. I call it dream alchemy. Here's what to do.

As an example, imagine a dream of a little dog, trapped in a tiny enclosure with no room to run and be happy. This kind of dream comes up when you feel trapped, with no real freedom to express yourself and be happy. Perhaps you have set limits in your life, or put up a barrier to keep yourself in a comfort zone instead of facing your fears and daring to do and be more.

To turn around your dream and your life, in this example, a dream alchemy practice is to visualise, while you are awake, letting that little dream dog run and play in a big, open field. Make sure you feel really happy for the little dream dog as you do this.

Repeat 20 times a day for two weeks, and something quite magical will happen. You will notice you feel happier, and less trapped, and life will deliver some awesome surprises. (Adapt to suit your dream.)

For magical outcomes, do your dream alchemy

Tip 91
Bring it on!

hen a dream shows you a wonderful, uplifting, positive symbol, you can use it to spin a little dream alchemy to accelerate the manifestation of excellent outcomes into your life.

There are many tips throughout this book describing how to transform a negative aspect of a dream into a positive one by visualising the change over and over again. For example, if you dreamed of a little bird, trapped and unable to fly high, and related your dream to feeling trapped in your career, you can visualise the little bird freed from its trap, flying free and high. What this visualisation does is communicate with your unconscious mind, using its own symbolic language, to change those unconscious beliefs that have been stopping you from flying high in your career.

But remember, what dreams do is process your experiences of the last 24–48 hours to update your view of the world and your place in it. In this way, they are the blueprint of your future, as the future is most likely to turn out according to your beliefs and experiences. Now, imagine something happens at work to give you a glimpse of what it would be like to fly high in your career, to feel free instead of trapped. Your dream might process this experience into a dream of a resplendent bird flying high, up and far away from where it had been trapped. Such a dream would suggest your beliefs are changing, that you are beginning to see that there is nothing holding you back from flying high.

That being so, how long are you going to wait for this belief to fully form? This is where the dream alchemy practice comes in. By simply visualising this positive part of the dream—the resplendent bird flying high, up and far away from where it had been trapped —and making sure you add uplifting feelings of joy, freedom, and ease to the visualisation—you can consolidate your new belief and accelerate its manifestation in your life.

What will you manifest in this example? A sudden insight that the trap was all of your own making, an opportunity to fly high and, possibly, some synchronicities in the shape of resplendent birds and high flying symbols awesomely peppering your days.

Pump up the positive symbols in your dreams

Tip 92
Your solution is between the opposites

ere's a great tip for when you're feeling stuck and need some guidance to move forward. Most dreams, when you look at them closely, have at least one pair of opposites. Your dream might involve slow and fast, or high and low, or noisy and quiet, or long way round and short way round. Look for these opposites, and write them down.

If the opposites don't jump out at you straight away, look at the personalities of any people in your dream. Dreams usually highlight people with opposite personalities or approaches to life. For example, one person in your dream might be someone you consider very flexible and open-minded, while another person in the same dream might be someone you consider rigid and closed-minded. Not all dreams contain pairs of opposites, but most do, so have a really good look.

When you find a pair of opposites, ask which opposite best describes you or a life experience you are encountering right now. Then ask what you think about people who tend to be in the opposite corner from you on this. Finally, ask if you were ever in that opposite corner before you 'swapped sides'.

These pairs of opposites define issues that your dream is processing. Something is only an issue in your life if you tend towards one extreme (or corner) because you find something about the other extreme uncomfortable. For example, you might tend towards being too flexible because you haven't had good experiences with rigid people and don't want to be like them. Or you might tend towards being too rigid because being too flexible in the past seems to have created difficulties for you.

What's the solution? The solution is to identify the issue (in this example, the issue is how flexible or how rigid to be about something in your life right now) and then to balance your approach by finding a mid-point between the two extremes. For example, it's usually best in any situation to take an approach about halfway between too flexible and too rigid, a place where a bit of both serves you well.

Dreams help you to identify issues you have been blind to, issues that are affecting your life in a negative way. They help you to see where your life needs more balance. It's up to you to follow that cue.

Also see Tip 48

Discover the formula for balance and harmony

Tip 93
How to seek an answer from your dreams

ince dreams are so good at processing your experiences, revealing your hidden beliefs and feelings, and coming up with creative solutions to problems, can you program a dream to investigate a problem or question, and come up with a possible solution?

Yes, you can. It's a process known as dream incubation. It works like this.

Your dreams process your experiences of the last two days, but special emphasis is put on any problem you have been focussing on during the day that is also on your mind as you fall asleep. There's your simple formula. This is what to do.

Write down the problem you would like to solve in your dreams, framing it as a question. Make your question as precise as you can. For example, "What next step do I need to take to attract a publisher to publish my book?" or "How can I make my monthly bookkeeping easier?" or "How can I promote my business on a budget of $x a week?" or "What do I need to change within myself to attract my perfect partner?"

Don't even think of not writing your question down. You may think you know exactly what you're asking your dream to solve, but it will be too loose for your dream to address precisely until you formulate it in writing. Also, when you wake in the morning, you need to be able to compare the symbols in your dream to your exact question.

Write your question down early in the day, and read it at least once every half-hour. Plan a quiet, relaxed evening, with very little stimulation. Remember, you don't want your dreaming mind to pick up any other topic from your evening to explore. Listen to peaceful music, have a long bath, do some mundane but relaxing household chores.

Make sure going to bed is a quiet, peaceful process. Keep the lights in your bedroom low. You might like to have a special pillow, or incense you use only for dream incubation nights. Your only permitted reading material is your dream incubation question that you must read twenty times before closing your eyes. Then keep repeating the question in your mind as you drift off to 'sleep on it'.

You may wake up with an answer that feels right before even interpreting your dreams. If so, write it down. Then examine your dreams. Don't expect a literal answer. Dreams are symbolic, even when responding to dream incubation questions, so use the tips throughout this book to interpret their response. (Note: As dreams address issues from the last 24-48 hours, don't be surprised if your solutions are reserved for the second night.)

Tip 94
How to change the world through your dreams

hen you're dreaming, you think the dream is for real, don't you? When you wake up, you're surprised to find that your dream didn't happen. When you're awake, you know that you also experience a dream reality, but when you're asleep, you don't know that you also experience a waking reality. The dream is it, your total reality, while you're in it.

Does this thought ever make you question your waking reality? It should. How real is waking life if dreaming life, while you're in it, also seems real? Might you one day wake up from waking life and discover it, too, was a kind of dream?

Your experience of waking life is a result of how you see it: both how you choose to see life, and how your unconscious mind sees it. We all look at life from our own personal perspectives. We all experience the same world from different angles. We all process and interpret the world we live in according to our beliefs, attitudes, and previous experiences.

So how real is the waking world you experience? Is it a kind of dream? You decide. It's definitely a kind of illusion, isn't it? It's your illusion, and you can change it at any point by changing the way you see it. Dream interpretation helps you to understand and see through your own illusions. In this way, dream interpretation helps you to change your waking world. The tip here is that the best way to change the world is to start with your dreams. As you get to understand yourself deeply, you start to see how the world can become a better place, and how you can play your part in its transformation. Begin with learning how to interpret your dreams.

Understand and see through your illusions

Tip 95
Using dreams to heal and ease disease

an dreams help you to heal from disease? Most, if not all, diseases begin with the mind. Stress, emotional issues, fears, and beliefs can and do manifest in the physical body if not addressed. When your mind is not at ease, when it is at dis-ease, bodily disease may follow. Since dreams reveal your emotional and mental make-up, they offer an opportunity to understand a disease or illness from an emotional-mental perspective.

If you are prone to sickness, or suffering a disease, look through your dreams for symbolic representations of your physical condition. For example, you might see a balloon about to burst under pressure when you're suffering a headache, a stack of bricks out of alignment when your spine is out of line, a cloudy or murky pond when you've got a bladder infection, an off-key or raspy musical instrument when you've got a throat infection, a blocked road or pipe when you've got a blockage such as a blocked artery or constipation, a toxic waste factory polluting a system when you've got a liver or kidney problem, or an invasion or war dream when your immune system is fighting an infection.

These are NOT definite symbols with strict meanings, as any of these symbols can come up in dreams that have nothing to do with physical disease, so don't use these to diagnose your physical condition. Instead, use these examples as guidelines to help you identify parts of your dream that seem to mirror your physical condition.

Once you've found your personal symbol of your disease in a dream, the healing magic begins with a dream alchemy practice. This is what to do.

Visualise the dream situation healing, adding an uplifting emotion. For example, visualise a blocked pipe unblocking, and its contents flowing smoothly, feeling the elation of the release. Or visualise the high-pressure balloon that was about to burst breathing out gently, just enough to relieve the pressure, and feel the light-hearted, happy balloon lift and fly. Or visualise the stack of bricks being gently stretched and reset into alignment, feeling the joyous freedom of a new flexibility.

Keep up your visualisation for several weeks, always making sure to add and feel that uplifting emotion. What you are doing is communicating with your unconscious mind using its own language, the language of your dreams. Your unconscious mind then takes your healing cue, and helps heal the emotional or mental cause of your dis-ease by changing the disease-causing beliefs and feelings. Watch your dreams for feedback on your healing progress.

Tip 96
A dream guide to a safe bet

Should you rush off and bet numbers that come up in dreams on the lottery, horse races, or roulette? Well, some overnight millionaires will urge 'yes' based on their experiences, but many other people will advise you to hold onto your money and become infinitely richer through interpreting your dream to discover the significance of those dream numbers.

Understanding the meaning of a number in your dream can be life changing in a positive, enriching, rewarding way. So what's the secret?

First up, remove any zeroes. Dreams add zeroes for drama—2,000,000 looks much more exciting than 2 or 20. A number in a dream usually refers to a time period OR to an age. The number 5 in your dream might draw your attention to five years ago, or when you were five, for example. Dreams are not rigid though, so also look for five months or five weeks ago. You'll always find a surprising connection to the rest of your dream, and sigh a deep 'Aha'.

Understanding the meaning of a number in your dream can be life changing

Tip 97
A guide to life's highways and byways

ill you arrive at your destination? Car travel dreams are usually about your progress—or lack of it—in achieving a goal in your life. You know where you want to be, but how goes the journey? What obstacles are you meeting along the way? Things that hold you back in your dream reflect things that are holding you back in life.

Got a flat tyre? Ask where you're feeling flat, running out of buoyancy. Is the windscreen misty or dirty? Ask where your goal seems to be unclear, or where your vision of the goalposts is fading. Can't get into the right gear? Where is this happening in your life, metaphorically speaking? Is the engine overheating? Ask where you're pushing yourself too hard, and take the cue from your dream that slogging on could lead to burnout.

Do your brakes fail? What, you can't stop? Where in your life do you need to stop and rest, or slow down before you hit the wall? Do you crash? Oops, have you already 'crashed' in some area of your life, or are you heading that way?

Is the road ahead running out? Ask if you've outrun your goals, lost your way, can't stop driving yourself, or need to set new goals. Is your dream car heading over the edge of a cliff road, about to fall? Then ask if you've really driven yourself to the edge—and possibly beyond—or whether it's time for you to leave the road you had planned, take a risk, and fly!

Is your dream car out of control? What feels out of control in your life? If your dream car is out of control, and the more you tighten your grip on the wheel and try to steer the vehicle straight, the more out of control the car gets, then ask where in your life today you fear losing control so much that you're holding on too tight, being too controlling to allow for the kind of flexibility needed to achieve real success. If this is your recurring dream, help yourself overcome your control issues by visualising loosening your grip on the wheel, providing firm direction while allowing the universe to play its part in steering you towards achieving your goal.

Also see Tips 29, 30, 61

Let the universe play its part

Tip 98
The message or the messenger?

How well does your mobile phone work in dreams? Is it hard to punch the keys, or do you keep forgetting the number you want to call? Does the person you're calling never pick up? Or do you lose your mobile phone, and spend most of your dream searching for it?

Decades ago, this very common dream might have involved landline phones, or looking for public phones or telephone kiosks. Roll back a few decades more and you might have dreamed of your ink running out whenever you wanted to write a letter, or a sudden snowstorm preventing all mail coach deliveries. Further back in history such dreams probably revolved around messenger boys getting ambushed or would-be lovers returning letters with the wax seal unbroken. Thousands of years back, the dreamer might not have been able to signal his hunting partner because … you've got the picture.

Dream symbols may change throughout history, but some dilemmas stay the same, and the dilemma here is communication.

Symbols can change. Look beyond the symbol to the dynamics of a dream. The dynamics of most mobile phone dreams involve communication, or lack of it. If you're failing to get through to someone in a dream, ask where in your waking life you feel you are failing to get a message across. Then ask if your own inner communication systems could be failing. Are your head and heart working together or separately? Does your right hand know what your left hand is doing? Are you efficient and co-ordinated in the way you handle life, or does your life seem to be the result of a bunch of mixed messages acquired from childhood?

Tone up your communication efficiency by doing this dream alchemy practice when you wake from this dream. Visualise yourself back in the dream, only this time make the connection. Locate your mobile phone easily, get the number right, and talk to the other person clearly. When you do this, pump up the positive feelings: feel happy and uplifted about communicating so easily, and about your message being heard and accepted. Repeat this visualisation throughout the day, and for weeks to come. Your unconscious mind will follow suit, and the communication issue will naturally resolve.

Dream symbols may change throughout history

Tip 99
Guidance in a hurry

I s there a shortcut method you can use to interpret a dream when you're in a hurry? To interpret a whole dream, no, but here's a quick and simple method you can use to get a wonderful nugget of meaningful insight. This is what to do.

Write one short sentence summarising your dream in the present tense, starting with the words 'I feel' and including the word 'something'. Then ask, "Where does this apply in my life?" and see what comes up.

Here are some examples.

Your dream

My son was carrying a stack of precious, fine china crockery. We were moving house, and I was worried that the china should have been properly packed to prevent it from breaking.

Summary sentence

I feel worried that something precious and fragile may break.

In my life

I feel worried that my relationship is precious and fragile and may break, and I now see this is affecting the way I act towards my partner.

Your dream

I have a plane to catch, but everything goes wrong, and I never get airborne.

Summary sentence

I feel frustrated that so many delays are slowing me down from achieving something so simple.

In my life

I feel frustrated that I never reach my target weight because my family and friends feel offended if I don't eat the cakes they keep baking for me: why don't I just say no?

Your dream

I saw a huge beehive, and started to climb into it, at the same time thinking this was dangerous and I'd be stung. I saw rows and rows of golden honey, and ate some. To my surprise, I didn't get hurt.

Summary sentence

I feel surprise that when I dive into something I think will be painful I discover such rich rewards.

In my life

I was surprised when I agreed to take on a difficult project last week and I learned so much from the experience: why don't I do this more often?

Give it a go. You'll be surprised at how much insight this method delivers. What's that? Can't stop, no time for dream interpretation, you've a plane to catch? I don't think so.

Tip 100
Let the magic happen

As you work through recording and interpreting your dreams, you can sometimes feel a little bogged down in writing and thinking.

Counteract this by creating a dream corner, or dream alchemy alcove, in your home. Make this a beautiful uplifting space dedicated to inspiring your dream goals and dream alchemy practices.

Decorate your chosen area with artwork, pictures, fabrics, colours, and ornaments that represent positive symbols from your dreams and visualisations. If you are doing a visualisation transforming a wilting tree from a dream into a healthy, flowering, fruiting tree, for example, decorate your dream corner with pictures of trees in flower and fruit, place a big bowl of fresh fruit on a shelf or small table, and add a few drops of blossom or fruit essence to an incense burner.

If you have room, add a chair or cushion so you can take time out to relax or meditate, surrounded by the very symbols that are transforming your life while reminding you of your intention.

Let the ambience embrace and uplift you. Aim to spend at least five minutes every day in this magical space.

Spend at least five minutes every day in this magical space

Tip 101
Start a dream group

nce you've mastered the 101 tips in this book, consider yourself graduated from 'Dream Interpretation 101'. Congratulations! It's time to start practising, and that's what this final tip is all about.

Many of these tips are multi-tipped, power-packed with information, techniques, and exercises that you will want to revisit over and over again as you fine-tune your dream interpretation skills. It may be a slim volume, but it's a rich resource. If you count the tips within tips you may decide that '1,001 Dream Interpretation Tips' is a more apt title.

So here it is. Tip 101 or Tip 1,001! Start a Dream Group. This is what to do.

Invite up to four people to form a dream group, and meet once a week to discuss your dreams. Make it easy on yourself by using this book as your guide. Purchase a copy for each member, or ask members to buy copies because they will need to study it between sessions. The idea is to share dreams, help each other with interpretations, support and motivate each other in doing the visualisations and other exercises, and celebrate the results.

You will probably have plenty of ideas about how to organise your dream group. At each meeting, you might choose to focus in depth on just one person's dream, or you might each want to discuss a dream more generally. Alternatively, you might want to simply introduce a topic at each meeting, perhaps a chapter or individual tip from this book. Each member of the group can study the chapter or tip in the preceding week and bring in an example of one of their own dreams on the topic to share.

The possibilities are endless. Make sure that no one imposes an interpretation on anyone else. A dream group is about sharing and guiding, not preaching or counselling. Help each dreamer to explore their dream by asking them questions guided by the tips in this book. Remember that each dream symbol is unique and personal, so respect dreamers' feelings about what their dreams mean to them.

It can be difficult to see the meaning of your own dream when you are too close to the issues involved, and so rewarding to reach that 'Aha' of recognition about your dream when the right person asks you the right question at the right time.

Are you ready to begin? Pick up the phone …

Tip 102
A healthy sleep

The Wenatex Sleep System

Quality dreams need quality sleep. They go hand in hand. And because I deeply treasure both, I want to recommend simply the best sleep system you'll ever encounter. It's revolutionary and completely different to any other sleep system. And it's deliciously and sensuously comfortable while doing extraordinary things for your health in outstandingly clever ways.

So now that you know how impressed I am with this system and the way it benefits both sleep and dreams, you'll understand why I invited Wenatex's professional sleep specialists to provide a bonus tip for this book. I've also included their contact details so you can discover more about getting the best quality sleep and dreams from all those years you spend asleep—that's around 27 years for the average life expectancy!

For all the reasons you will read below, I am sincerely grateful to Wenatex for everything they have done, and continue to do, in the cause of healthy sleep and the kind of quality dreams that add meaning to our lives.

I wish you Sweet Dreams, and farewell you with my final tip, which is to equip yourself with the best sleeping conditions in which to dream. Why suffer broken, fitful dreams when you can experience uninterrupted, high quality dreams every night? I hand you over to Wenatex's professional sleep specialists for the rest of this tip.

—Jane Teresa

It is essential that we not only get the right quantity of sleep, but also the right quality of sleep. It is possible to sleep for eight hours and still wake up feeling tired. It's also possible to have a 20-minute afternoon nap and wake feeling completely refreshed. So what makes the difference?

You fall asleep in stages—five stages to be exact. Stage 1 is where you cross from consciousness to your unconscious sleep stage. During Stage 2, you are asleep, but can be easily woken up again—you are lightly asleep. In Stage 3, you begin to fall into a deeper level of sleep, and by Stage 4 your breathing has slowed, your heart rate has dropped, and your body has cooled. Stage 4 is where your body produces natural Human Growth Hormone. This stage is extremely important, as it is during this time that your body heals and regenerates cells. After about 90 minutes, you move into Stage 5—the REM, or Rapid Eye Movement sleep stage. During this stage, your mind becomes hyperactive and, of course, you begin to dream. Stage 5 is all-important as this is the time your mind reconciles thoughts, filters information, and stores memories.

During a normal sleep, your body runs through approximately 4–5 cycles per night—moving from Stage 1 to 2 to 3 to 4 and then to 5, then back to 4 then 3, before going back to 4 and to 5—and so on. If you are able to follow this natural sleep cycle all the way throughout the night, you will be sure to wake in the morning feeling 100% fresh and ready to take on the day.

However, there are both external and internal influences that can interrupt your natural sleep cycle. External influences commonly include crying babies, barking dogs, or bright street lamps. Internal influences include acute or chronic pain, over-heating, partner disturbance, asthma, and sleep pathologies such as sleep apnoea.

The goal for each and every one of us is to do everything within our power to reduce these potential interruptions. Suggestions include, improving your baby's routine, wearing ear plugs, or installing opaque curtains to make the room as dark as possible.

Unfortunately, once you have taken care of the issues outside the confines of your bed, there are still many other things that can cause interruptions under the sheets. Partner disturbance, poor sleep posture, a snoring partner, sneezing and dust allergies are some of the critical issues facing each of us every night, minimising our chances of having that great restorative sleep and those high-quality, uninterrupted dreams.

You're going to be asleep for 27 years of your life, and it's essential that these years are as healthy as possible.

Our company, Wenatex, founded more than 40 years ago in Germany, and now spread throughout Europe, Australia and New Zealand, created a Sleep System (a mattress, quilt, pillow and slat base) to address all the bed-related issues that can produce interrupted sleep.

The Wenatex Sleep System addresses sleep hygiene, sleep posture, over-heating, and partner disturbance. The product is tested free from harmful chemicals and, as an option, even introduces the benefits of aromatherapy, utilising herbs such as eucalyptus, lavender, and shepherds' purse, to name a few. All our bedding products are guaranteed for five years, are delivered and installed into most homes for free, and our customer support team is on hand in case of queries in relation to the product or your sleep in general.

If you want to be more productive, make more money, look younger, and feel healthier, you need to ensure your sleep environment is as healthy as possible. So take advantage of this Dream Tip 102 and equip yourself with the best sleep conditions in which to dream—you will be rewarded with a great night's sleep every night.

If you are interested in learning more about our healthy Sleep System, or would like an <u>obligation free</u> demonstration, please contact our team.

Wenatex Australia Pty Ltd
Free Call: 1800 006 606
Email: info@wenatex com.au
Web: dreamtip102.wenatex.com.au

Wenatex New Zealand Limited
Free Call: 0800 006 606
Email: info@wenatex.co.nz
Web: dreamtip102.wenatex.co.nz

FURTHER READING

Jane Teresa Anderson *Dream Alchemy*, 2nd ed Hachette Livre 2007

——*The Shape of Things to Come*, Random House 1998

——*Dream It: Do It!* Harper Collins, 1995

——*Sleep On It*, Harper Collins, 1994

E-books, free resources and articles: www.dream.net.au

INDEX

By the same author
A companion guide

Dream Alchemy
Jane Teresa Anderson

The complete list of common dream themes and their meanings, with magical dream alchemy practices to transform your life.

Identify your most common dream themes—themes you share with millions of others—then apply the dream alchemy practices given for each dream theme to create positive life change.

Included is information about how to:

- Stop uncomfortable recurring dreams
- Identify emotional obstacles and release them
- Create more fulfilling relationships
- Discover your talents and life purpose
- Heal the past
- Work with the emotions and feelings in your dreams
- Transform fearful dreams into loving visions
- Tap into your creative source
- Identify your spiritual lessons and move forward
- Use your dreams to strike personal and spiritual gold
- Design your own dream alchemy practices

Jane Teresa Anderson *Dream Alchemy*, 2nd ed, Hachette Livre, 2007

Available from all good bookshops or from www.dream.net.au

Dream
Alchemy

❧ the ULTIMATE GUIDE ❧
to interpreting your dreams

JANE TERESA ANDERSON

Discuss your dreams with me

Confidential consultations
By phone
By email
In person

Details: www.dream.net.au